Writing your first clinical research protocol

Writing your first clinical research protocol

Colleen Aldous
Paul Rheeder
Tonya Esterhuizen

JUTA

Writing your first clinical research protocol
First published 2011
Reprinted May 2012
Reprinted February 2013
Reprinted 2015 (twice)

Juta and Company Ltd
1st Floor, Sunclare Building, 21 Dreyer Street, Claremont, 7708
PO Box 14373, Lansdowne, 7779, Cape Town, South Africa

© 2013 Juta & Company Ltd

ISBN 978-0-70218-894-7

All rights reserved. No part of this publication may be reproduced or transmitted in any form or by any means, electronic or mechanical, including photocopying, recording, or any information storage or retrieval system, without prior permission in writing from the publisher. Subject to any applicable licensing terms and conditions in the case of electronically supplied publications, a person may engage in fair dealing with a copy of this publication for his or her personal or private use, or his or her research or private study. See Section 12(1)(a) of the Copyright Act 98 of 1978.

Publisher: Sarah O'Neill
Project Manager: Corina Pelser
Editor: Alfred Le Maitre
Proofreader: Simone van der Merwe
Typesetter: ANdtp Services, Cape Town
Typeset in: 10.5pt on 13pt Optima
Indexer: Hannelie Knoetze
Cover designer: Nikki Richardson
Printed and bound by Castle Graphics South (Pty) Ltd

The author and the publisher believe on the strength of due diligence exercised that this work does not contain any material that is the subject of copyright held by another person. In the alternative, they believe that any protected pre-existing material that may be comprised in it has been used with appropriate authority or has been used in circumstances that make such use permissible under the law.

'I believe that a scientist should be judged by the quality of the people he has helped to produce and not by prizes or other honours bestowed on him. Let my works speak for themselves.'

Sydney Brenner

Table of contents

WIIFM: What's in it for me?.	1
Finding your research focus.	5
Creating research problem statements and defining your aims and objectives.	11
Conducting the literature review.	18
Selecting an appropriate study design.	24
Measurement.	30
Research participant selection.	34
Ethics and ethical approval.	40
The data collection instrument.	43
Limitations of the research.	45
Preparing your plan for data analysis.	47
Budgets and timelines.	57
The research title and your title page.	63
The executive summary.	68
Reporting your findings and establishing authorship.	74
References and appendices.	78
Bibliography.	81
Appendix A: An example of a protocol template.	82
Index.	87

WIIFM: What's in it for me?

The research component of your degree exists because it has been shown over the history of medical research that graduates, including you, will derive significant professional benefits from doing research. For most postgraduate clinical students, research is not a priority when they register. They want to get stuck into doing the work in the wards and get on with their clinical training, and they often see the research project as a pointless hurdle! Contrary to the belief some have, the research project was not invented to make your life more difficult than it currently is or to satisfy the whims of sadistic academics. In addition, there may be career benefits; for certain positions within the public sector, preference could be given to clinicians with postgraduate research experience and publications.

We want to make the process of writing up your first research protocol a breeze. We have taken into account that you are under a lot of pressure and work unenviable hours, so in this book we have broken the process down into smaller, instructive bite-size pieces that you can work through in short bursts of time.

What will you gain professionally by doing a research project?

Here are some of the areas of potential growth, or strengths you could gain, as a clinician by doing research:

- You will learn how to *ask a focused question* aimed at improving medical practice. Without carrying out independent research, a clinician is happy to just get up to speed, or up to date. However, independent research teaches you to think critically and ask questions that could actually expand the current knowledge base about aetiology, diagnosis or therapy.
- You will learn how to use large medical databases for your *literature review*. With this experience you will be able to find relevant literature when faced with anomalies, or when you become interested in other aspects of your discipline.
- You will learn how to review a lot of material in an *efficient* manner as well as how to *critically appraise the literature*. With this wisdom, you will be able to choose diagnostic and therapeutic tools based on best evidence.
- You will gain some understanding regarding *study designs* and *biostatistics*. This is essential knowledge if you want to read current research literature to keep up to date with the latest research.
- You will learn the art of *concise scientific writing*.

Writing your first clinical research protocol

- You will understand and implement *measurement methods*, ensuring accuracy and validity; skills that are as vital in clinical practice as they are in research.
- You will develop *presentation skills* when you get the opportunity to present your research protocol and your research findings.
- Most projects foster *interdependence*. You are always dependent on other team members (the laboratory, other departments and other clinical colleagues). This helps you to become a good team player.

Exercise

Take five minutes and write down five benefits you think you could derive from doing a research project. Do not repeat the above list, but be specific to your own context.

1. _____

2. _____

3. _____

4. _____

5. _____

Major constraints you will have to overcome

In some cases, clinical departments focus largely on teaching and clinical service delivery, with very little emphasis given to research. This means that a number of the three main requirements for a good research project are often lacking. These are:

1. *Adequate time* allocated to research activity: Most often you will be expected to do your project as part of your usual clinical practice.
2. *Adequate funding:* Small projects often don't form part of a large funded project.
3. *Adequate mentoring:* At times, clinical consultants or supervisors are very busy and not available for adequate mentoring, or are themselves inexperienced in research activity.

WIIFM: What's in it for me?

These constraints could, of course, severely restrict what is feasible, and what is not, in terms of what you can research. The challenge is to find creative ways to overcome these obstacles without sacrificing quality or relevance. It may be to your advantage to determine which flagship funded projects are currently being carried out in your department. There may be a component that is suitable as a sub-study for you to complete.

What are some of the constraints you will have to overcome?

> *Exercise*
>
> There may be more constraints applicable to your research context. List three challenges that you think are most relevant for you.
>
> 1. _____
> 2. _____
> 3. _____

How to make a start on developing your protocol

Writing a good protocol is fundamentally your blueprint for accomplishing the research project. However, you do not write the protocol only for yourself. You write the protocol to convince other people (such as those on academic and ethics committees or funding bodies) of the scientific value and need for your research. Essentially, all the readers of your protocol will have the same needs:

- They will need to be put in the picture with regard to the context of your study.
- They will want to know what it is you intend to discover through your research.
- They will want to know how you will go about finding out what you want to find out. In other words, are your methods appropriate for the question you are asking?
- They will want to know that you have taken into consideration everything that is required for your clinical research.

Some institutions use a template that has been tried and tested by many other successful researchers to ensure that a protocol contains all the required elements. An example of a template can be found in Appendix A at the end of this book. Templates may differ slightly from one institution to the next, but there are elements common to all protocols. The rest of this workbook covers each element of a protocol in detail. Much of writing up a protocol is an iterative process, with movement forwards and backwards as you think around the topic with more

Writing your first clinical research protocol

clarity. We have covered the elements in more or less the way you will go about working on them, and not in the order that they will appear in your final research protocol document.

> *Learning points*
>
> There are a number of clear personal advantages when you plan and execute a research project successfully. Being sure of these helps you to complete your project with enthusiasm. However, you have to understand the limitations of time, funding and research supervision, and find creative ways to overcome these.

Finding your research focus

Many students are daunted by the need to come up with a research topic to investigate. After reading this chapter, you will hopefully have dozens of research ideas buzzing around in your mind.

Finding a research focus area in which to work is driven by curiosity, opportunity, need or profit, or a combination of two or more of these. Curiosity-driven research has been within the ambit of academia for centuries, but with research costs spiralling and research funding becoming scarce, research that is driven by need or profit will provide more opportunities.

Some first-time researchers may find themselves within a research group with research ideas already defined by the principal investigator. It may be a good idea to seek out a research group that you are interested in working with so that you can contribute to the larger body of research that is being coordinated within such a group.

For the most part, you will need to come up with your own research ideas. Technically, you can study anything you are interested in. You are already registered within a specialist discipline you enjoy working in, and which will define the broad area in which you will carry out your research. Find a topic within this area to research that will motivate you and will extend medical science knowledge. You may already have a specific idea from your experience that you would like to take further, or you may have to spend some time thinking about what you would like to research.

Sources of research ideas

Research problems can abound on a daily basis if you are curious and observant.

- In your daily practice, whenever you ask yourself *why something has happened*, you have a potential research problem.

    Example: Why is it that the MDR-TB patients in my hospital are not responding to their treatment?

- Or you may identify *problems* in your daily practice that may need a solution.

    Example: My patients are not taking their ARVs correctly. We must find a way of making it easier for them to take their meds. Maybe we should combine different medications into a single capsule or tablet?

- Ask yourself why you sometimes observe things *contrary to the literature*.

    Example: I am interested in renal disease in the paediatrics ward. One of the conditions I see is the nephrotic syndrome (NS). Some of my patients are not responding to therapy that is seen as the standard. I read a paper in a medical journal that shows that children with NS respond to steroids. But these are Caucasian children and my patients are black and Indian. I conducted an audit and found that Indian children responded to steroids (85% of them) but the black children just battled — no response, along with hypertension and severe steroid side effects (only 15% responded). I will look at biopsies of all children with NS. That will be the basis of my research.

This brings up the next source of research ideas: the literature. Read about your field in academic journals, professional magazines, theses and appropriate online sites; see what other researchers in your area of interest have studied already. Not only can you discover alternative findings in your own context, but the literature also provides interesting questions that could be asked again in your context; you may replicate some research if you anticipate you could find something different within the community in which you work. For example, there may be a genetic problem in the Caucasian population that causes lactic acidosis in patients on HAART and which may or may not occur in the Zulu population, which has a higher frequency of lactic acidosis on HAART.

- *Published articles* often highlight areas for further research. In the discussion and conclusion sections of many articles, the authors will highlight the limitations of their research as well as questions that arise as a result of their work. You can take on a study that starts where their studies finish off, or you can repeat their study, addressing some of the limitations. Technology moves ahead very quickly, and some older research topics may be better answered currently with the use of better technology. Review articles are a gold mine of ideas; they cover the research in various aspects of an area and also highlight the gaps in the research, where you could find excellent opportunities for research.
- A couple of hours spent browsing through *Google Scholar* (www.scholar.google.com) will open up a treasure-trove of ideas for your research focus. One student had an idea about looking into the experiences of female carriers of haemophilia, but did not know how to narrow her study down to a specific question. She wrote the phrase 'experiences of female carriers of haemophilia' into the search box and got 3 550 articles in less than a second, from professional journal articles to blogs. Browsing through the list, she found she could look at various focus areas, such as:
    - ❏ carrier testing for haemophilia;
    - ❏ prenatal diagnosis of haemophilia;
    - ❏ obstetric and gynaecological issues in haemophilia carriers;

- clinical management of haemophilia carriers;
- genetic counselling issues specific to haemophilia carriers and their families; or
- community attitudes and beliefs around haemophilia carriers.

Within 10 minutes, she had six focus areas where she could carry out research specific to haemophilia carriers in her clinic.

- Another invaluable source for research ideas is your *interaction with others* who are also interested in your broader area. Speak to, interact with and ask advice from peers and mentors within your department. Novice researchers can learn a lot from experienced researchers, particularly that which is not written down in the texts you will read. If you have the opportunity, attend conferences and other scientific meetings in your area. At conferences, you will be able to interact with other people outside your institution who are doing research in your area. You will be able to see the trends in research in your area and possibly formulate collaborations with other experts.

How to find your own research focus

Several examples are given above for methods of finding a research focus. If you are completely baffled about where to start, the following order of actions will help you to home in on a research topic of your own:

1. Speak to your supervisor and get some idea about what research area he or she is already interested in. By researching within a team, you will have access to a lot of research expertise in the area to help you along the way. Your supervisor may advise you to study something other than what you had in mind, but it will be something that he or she is interested in and will therefore be keen to support you.
2. Do a keyword search in Google Scholar and establish the scope of research that has been done in the area. Look at the first 10 or so pages of resources and see if you can see patterns in the research, much like the student above who wanted to look at haemophilia in carriers.
3. Download some of the materials that will be most relevant to your study. Check the dates of publication to make sure that you are as up to date as possible with your reading. Also, see how often the articles were cited; this will give you a good idea of who the leaders are in research in your focus area.
4. Observe your clinical surroundings. Take note of areas where your reading makes you notice things.
5. Interact with other leaders in the field and your colleagues within your group, as well as peers. There have been many serendipitous discussions in tearooms that have led to great research. Talk to lots of people about what you intend

Writing your first clinical research protocol

to research; you will be surprised how much feedback you will get that can inform your way forward.

> *Exercise*
>
> Write down a short statement that will give a broad indication of the area you would like to focus on for your research: for example, 'patterns of injuries in pick-up vehicle (bakkie) accidents'.
>
> *Nutrition support and wound healing*
>
> Go to Google Scholar and type your short statement into the search box. Write down how many items were returned and how long it took for the search to complete.
>
> *211 000*
>
> Spend some time looking at the first 10 pages of titles given. Write down the focus areas that you can identify.
>
> *Arginine*
> *Physiology of wound healing*
> *Route of nutrition support*
> *Timing of nutrition support*

Defining the research problem within your research area

Once you have identified a broad research idea, you have to find a narrow, focused *research(able) problem* within that area, one that you want to solve by doing your research project.

Defining the research problem helps you to clearly state what the identified gap in the current knowledge base is that you hope to address. Typically, the purpose of research is to find solutions to problems encountered in clinical practice (it could also, of course, be to decipher mechanisms in order to design new diagnostic tests or interventions). Once this is clear and concise, your research problem statement and aims and objectives follow logically.

Finding your research focus

Examples of good research problem statements
- Peripheral arterial disease (PAD) is common in patients with diabetes mellitus. Screening methods are time-consuming and operator-dependent. Identifying PAD with the help of a biomarker, or a combination of biomarkers, will be an advantage. B2 microglobulin (B2M) has been identified as one such possible marker, and needs further investigation in our patient population.
- Patients undergoing caesarean section using spinal anaesthesia have an increased risk of hypotension. It is still controversial whether crystalloid or colloids are most beneficial as preload/co-load. V……. is a new colloid used in our hospital. We would like to investigate its effect on blood pressure and heart rate in patients undergoing spinal anaesthesia for caesarean section.

Pitfalls to avoid
- *Do not write too much*: You will lose sight of the bigger picture and get bogged down in details if you write too much. Two to three paragraphs are sufficient.
- *Do not write too little*: You must paint a clear picture of the research problem to which your project is intended to find a solution.

Exercise

Having spent some time finding a focus area in the previous exercise, and having seen examples of good research problem definitions, write one to three paragraphs defining the problem you are going to investigate.

_____
_____
_____
_____
_____

Research focus checklist

Once you have decided on your research focus, but before you spend any time developing your research idea, see if you can answer 'yes' to each of the following points:

- Do you find the area you have chosen interesting, and will others in the research community also find it worthwhile?
- Are you sure your study has not been done before?
- Do you have the necessary skills to complete this research project? If not, are you able to acquire those skills or have access to people whom you could consult?

If you have to answer 'no' to any of these questions, go back to the drawing board. Once you have decided what your research focus will be, you will need to spend some time developing your research problem statement. The next section of this book goes into detail about how to develop a good research question or hypothesis.

Learning points

Although the task of finding a research idea may seem difficult to begin with, there are several sources of ideas for research that are easy to come by. You need to look around your work environment and spend some time looking at the literature, and soon you will have several ideas. Once you have a big picture of what you would like to study, you need to write down a short statement defining your research problem.

Creating research problem statements and defining your aims and objectives

Developing a good *research problem statement* is like taming a lion when it is a cub rather than waiting for it to become the head of a pride. You are now going to define your topic as a focused research problem statement (or *research statement* for short). As you begin thinking about doing a research project, it is all too easy to see too much of the bigger picture and put yourself off your research before you even start. We could invert a well-known adage to say that when you start your first research project, you may not be able to see the trees for the forest. To curb your distress, you need to develop a concise research statement, which could be in the form of either a *research question* or *hypothesis*, depending on the type of research you are going to do. This consists of a very short but detailed statement that affirms what you want to learn by doing your research. The research statement is the point of departure for the rest of your research project, and as such requires a lot of thought.

There are three good reasons why you must state your research problem as the first step in your research process:

1. In order to achieve smooth progress in your research, you have to start with a single-minded resolve to accomplish an outcome. In order to attain this kind of focus, you must define your research intention in the form of a research statement, which will define your protocol as you develop it. This statement will guide you continually to remain within the boundaries you set early on, so that you spend your time doing only what is required for your project and are able to meet your time requirements.
2. The research statement is your first step in developing your research plan. Used in presentations of your work, it will pique the interest of reviewers and will state clearly what you want to do and how you plan to go about achieving answers through your research.
3. Once you have refined your research statement, you will find it easier to locate specific and relevant information that will support your project. It will prevent you from becoming distracted by other interesting things and from collecting data which are not required to solve your particular research problem.

The research statement: research question or hypothesis?

Besides formulating the research statement clearly, this section is the *most important* of the whole protocol. *Be clear and concise.* What is it that you are attempting to do with this research project? This question may seem straightforward, but it is complicated by the fact that you have various options here.

The format in which you present your research statement will be determined by the type of project you are planning:

- *Descriptive studies* typically aim to answer a specific *question* or questions, such as: 'What is the prevalence of smoking among medical students?', or 'What is the positive and negative predictive value of the wiki test to diagnose meningitis?'
- *Analytical* studies, however, typically have *hypotheses* that you also want to test statistically, such as: 'Female students are more likely to smoke than males', or 'Exposing myocardial cells to high concentrations of calcium reduces post-ischaemic troponin levels.'

Because your choice of stating your research problem as either a research question or a hypothesis is based on the type of study you will be doing, it will not be required that you present your research statement as *both* a research question and a hypothesis. The two formats have a lot in common. Brevity and clarity are the key requirements for all research statements. Once you have your research idea, you can 'REFINE' it to get to a neat and tidy research statement. The mnemonic R-E-F-I-N-E can be used as a checklist to ensure a well-thought-out project proposal, and it can be adapted and applied to your research statement.

- **R**: Your research idea should be *relevant*, particularly to ensure funding and/or publication.
- **E**: The research you intend to embark upon must be *ethical*. Although ethical issues are very often dealt with separately later on in the setting up of your protocol, there are glaring ethical issues that can be identified right at the initial stages of thinking about your research.
- **F**: Ensure that your research intentions are *feasible*. At the very least you will have to take into consideration time, ethical and budgetary limitations when embarking upon a research project. Make sure you have all the resources required to measure the variables you need for your data in order to carry out your study. There is no point planning to look at the outcomes of a specific intervention where the intervention is rarely required: for example, studying the outcomes of regimen 1B ARV therapy in a clinic where the majority of patients are male and on regimen 1A.
- **I**: You are going to spend a lot of time doing this research, so it will help if the work is *interesting*. It should be interesting to you as well as the scientific community within your research area.

Creating research problem statements and defining your aims and objectives

- **N**: If possible, the research you do ought to be *novel*. It is always good to be able to say you have found out something that no one knew before.
- **E**: Your statement must be *epigrammatic*. This means that it must be short, fully informative and succinct. You will find that honing the statement down to be as specific as possible takes some time and is an iterative process. As you read in your area and interact with other researchers, your question will become more and more specific.

In business, the mnemonic S-M-A-R-T is often used as a checklist, too. After you have 'REFINE'd your research statement, you can 'SMART'en it up!

- **S**: Your statement must be *specific*.
- **M**: You must be able to define the variables that you will be *measuring* from your research statement.
- **A**: Your research must be *achievable*.
- **R**: Your research has to be *relevant*.
- **T**: Your project should be *testable*.

Exercise

What is wrong with these examples of research questions?

1. What is the true seroprevalence of HIV among the patients admitted to the Kakamas hospital with ………… trauma?
2. Will (and if so, how) this seroprevalence impact on the future management of patients admitted to the Department of …………………… in terms of:
   a) postoperative monitoring; and
   b) empiric antimicrobial therapy?

Write your thoughts in the space provided below:

_____

_____

_____

_____

_____

_____

Note: Refer to the end of this section for our suggestions on how to phrase research questions.

Writing your first clinical research protocol

How to do it yourself

Now that you have defined a focus area in which you are going to carry out your research, put some time aside to think more deeply about what you want to do. The process of developing a research statement may take no time at all if you have been thinking about what you want to do for some time already. However, it may take longer than anticipated, may be more painful and confusing than you thought it could be, and may at times feel a little lacking in direction.

Research statement checklist

1. Decide whether your research will be descriptive or analytical.
   Descriptive _____ Analytical _____
2. Will your research statement be in the form of a research question or a hypothesis? _____
3. State your research statement here:

   _____
   _____

4. Is your research statement REFINE'd and SMART?

Relevant	–	yes	no
Ethical	–	yes	no
Feasible	–	yes	no
Interesting	–	yes	no
Novel	–	yes	no
Epigrammatic	–	yes	no
Specific	–	yes	no
Measurable	–	yes	no
Achievable	–	yes	no
Relevant	–	yes	no
Testable	–	yes	no

5. If you answered 'no' to any of the above, go back to your statement and rework it until you can answer 'yes' to all points and you have a REFINE'd and SMART research statement.

Aims and objectives

The next step in developing your proposal is to state the research aims and objectives which emanate from the research problem statement. Many people have difficulty in differentiating between aims and objectives, and frankly, in normal use, there is not much that separates these two concepts. However, for the purposes of expounding a research problem statement, we can differentiate them as follows:

Aims are what you ultimately hope to achieve in your research project. The aim is a single overall statement that emphasises what you intend to accomplish, but not how you are going to go about doing it. There is often a single broad aim and other supporting secondary aims. There should be no more than five secondary aims to a primary aim.

Here is an example of a primary aim with one secondary aim:

- *Primary aim*: Compare the efficacy of Drug X versus Drug Y for lowering systolic blood pressure.
- *Secondary aim*: Compare the quality of life between the two treatment groups as measured with the SF36.

Exercise

Stating aims is easy. For your first attempt, start by looking at your research statement and then complete the following sentence:

The aim of my study is:

_____

_____

_____

If you have any secondary aims, list them here:

_____

_____

_____

_____

_____

Objectives are actions you need to do in order to achieve your aims. Objectives are a checklist of brief statements describing what you will do in order to meet the aim of the study. They are a list of numbered, focused statements that show the 'recipe' you are going to follow to get your anticipated research result.

Here is an example of aims and objectives statements for a single study:

The research question: How diagnostically accurate is B2 microglobulin (B2M) in detecting peripheral artery disease (PAD) in patients who have diabetes mellitus along with varying degrees of renal function?

Aim: To investigate the diagnostic accuracy of B2M to detect PAD in patients with diabetes mellitus and varying degrees of renal function.

Objectives: To establish the diagnostic characteristics of B2M to detect PAD as measured by the toe blood pressure index (TBI).

1. To determine the incremental diagnostic value of adding B2M to known cardiovascular risk factors for predicting PAD.
2. To determine whether the diagnostic value of B2M is modified by renal function, as measured by an estimated glomerular filtration rate (eGFR).

Pitfalls to avoid

- Sometimes the connection between the research statement and aims and objectives is not clear. Make sure there is a clear linear development of the research idea from the statement through to the aims and objectives. There should be no addition of aims and objectives that cannot be clearly read in the research statement.
- Sometimes the research idea is not measurable. Make sure you can define measurable variables from your research statement and include them in your aims and objectives.
- Avoid citing non-research objectives: for example, 'to make doctors aware of diabetes'. This should be under the heading of potential impact of the project and not under research objectives.

Exercise

Now write down your own objectives to your study. What is your approach? Do you need primary as well as secondary objectives?

_____

_____

Creating research problem statements and defining your aims and objectives

[blank lined box]

Aims and objectives checklist

- Are your aims and objectives clearly formulated and answerable?
- Are primary and secondary objectives needed?

Suggestions on the phrasing of research questions

Look again at the first exercise of this section. The first research question is answerable and measurable. The department could use the answer for health services planning (providing VCT, CD4 testing, appropriate referral, etc). On its own, however, it is not sufficient for a research dissertation.

The second research question is therefore very important. This question as phrased, however, is neither clear and concise nor measurable, and is therefore not answerable. How will they determine if 'this' seroprevalence impacts on future management? Do they really want to describe the differences in postoperative monitoring between HIV-positive and HIV-negative patients as seen in their setting? Their interest is to determine whether HIV status requires more (or less) comprehensive postoperative monitoring (and different empirical antimicrobial therapy). That would require the questions to be rephrased and the study design changed to an intervention study (rather than just a descriptive study).

Learning points

Once you have defined your area of interest, you have to collect your thoughts by defining a research problem statement, either as a hypothesis (for an analytical study) or as a research question (for a descriptive study). Once you have a succinct research problem statement, you can express the aim of your research (what you intend to do) and the objectives of your study (how you will achieve your aims).

Conducting the literature review

The literature review is an *original story* that you write that tells what has been happening in your field of interest. Simply put, you read a lot of literature around your research idea, think about what you have read, and then you write your own take on what has, and has not, been happening. You make a critical evaluation and synthesis of the research that has occurred in your area of interest and identify where there are evidence gaps.

The purpose of the literature review is twofold:

1. For you as a researcher, it serves to consolidate in your own mind what you have gleaned from the literature over time, clarifying your perspective on the research that has occurred in your area.
2. To others who read your literature review, it gives an idea of the context of your study and illustrates where there are gaps in the literature, giving them a clear idea of why you are going to do your research. It lends you credibility as a researcher by showing that you have read intensively and extensively and have a critical understanding of the research area; in other words, you know your area well.

Referencing (citing)

As you write, you need to acknowledge each author you refer to, by citing (the terms 'reference' and 'citation' are used interchangeably). This is called intellectual honesty. Failure to acknowledge other authors you quote or refer to constitutes one of the greatest academic sins, namely *plagiarism*.

The author or authors you quote or refer to are acknowledged both within the text where you refer to them and in the list of references at the end of your text. There are several different ways of going about this; these are called *referencing styles*. The humanities and the sciences use different referencing styles, but what all styles have in common is that they are rigid and very fixed. For most medical publications, the Vancouver system is used.

According to the Vancouver system, the citation within the text is indicated as a number that corresponds to the order in which the reference occurs in the writing, so the bracketed number (3) would indicate the third reference used in the writing. This reference would then occur in the list of references as the third in the list. In other styles, such as the Harvard style, the author's name and the year of publication will appear in the text. This affects the word count — something you need to remember, especially if you have been given a limited word count.

It is important to consult your instructions on the submission of your protocol to establish exactly which referencing style is required. Although in most cases the Vancouver style is used, the Harvard or the APA style can also be called for. You may be provided with examples and instructions on how to apply these styles; if not, the internet has many sources that can guide you. There is a well-designed online tutorial at www.lib.monash.edu.au/tutorials/citing/ covering most of the referencing styles used throughout academia. Incorrect referencing is probably one of the most common reasons for protocols being sent back to students.

Electronic management of your references

If you had to ask anyone who completed their studies in the previous century how they managed their literature sources, they would tell you how much time and energy went into it and how maddening it was to ensure that all citations within their text and reference list were correct after several rounds of revisions. Today the sweat has been taken out of this process. There are several software applications that will help you manage your resources on your computer and assist you in ensuring that your referencing style is correct throughout your writing. It is very likely that your institution has a licence for a referencing management package and that it is free for you to download. A chat with your librarian will clear this up for you. The most magical thing of all is that, say you have finished writing your entire protocol in the Harvard system because you like to see the name of the author you are citing in your text, your document can be changed to conform to the Vancouver style required for submission with a couple of clicks.

Writing up your own literature review

When you get a new cellphone, you read the instruction manual so that you can take full advantage of the features of the phone. When you plan a holiday, if you have the time, you could search websites that offer information about your destination, which may or may not impact how you will spend your time on that holiday. When you start research, you must look to the literature to inform you as to how to proceed with your research. Here are some pointers:

1. Seek out *only the relevant literature.* You will be able to receive training at your campus library on how to use the major online databases to search for academic literature. Look for literature that covers your research area broadly (but within the limits of your research idea) and then progressively narrow

down until you get to the specificity of your research statement where there is an inadequacy in the literature. Use the broad literature in a very limited way to set the scene, and then become more detailed as you approach your specific research statement. Less and less literature will be available as you narrow down your argument. And that is why you are putting your case forward to do the study.

2. Depending on the purpose of your review, it can include as few as six papers for a journal article (where you have only four paragraphs or so in which to achieve the purpose of the literature review) to several dozen for a dissertation. In the former, you have to cleverly show exactly why you did the study — almost like justifying your cause in a court of law — while in the latter, you can brag about how much you have read in the area. For a research protocol, you will need to write a maximum of three to four pages, and your aim is to put forward a case that justifies the reason for your study within a context. What is important is that all the material you read be relevant and specific to your area of research.

3. As you wade through the literature, organise the papers into different piles of commonality, and give titles to these piles. You can do this physically or on your computer by creating different folders. By doing this, you are organising the content of your literature review. You could have a pile (or folder) for papers with similar research aims, for others that use similar methods, for those that come to the same conclusions in different contexts, and for others that are inconsistent.

4. Once you have read enough to start writing your review, deal with the piles/folders one at a time, discussing the content in terms of relevance to your research. Draw attention to the shortfalls, if any, as well as the good and relevant points of the studies. The fact that something has been printed in an academic journal does not mean that it is faultless. Research methods move forward very quickly, and an article that exhibited state-of-the-art methods three years ago could now be shown to have deficiencies.

5. Structure the literature review as you would any good piece of writing, with an introduction, a body and a conclusion:

- The *introduction* provides broad context for the study.
- The *body* contains the literature in the various piles/folders of papers you have made.
- The *conclusion* contains the rationale and aims of the study. This is the 'so what?' statement, indicating how your study will take research in this area forward. It states how your study will build on work previously done, or in what way it is a new approach that may render more precise results.

Another way of looking at the literature review is as an inverse pyramid. Start broadly and then zoom in to where you have identified the gap that you will address. Here is an example of the proposed structure for a literature review on detecting peripheral arterial disease in patients with diabetes mellitus using a new biomarker:

1. Epidemiology of diabetes mellitus, highlighting that this is a common disease affecting many people (two to three paragraphs).
2. Long-term diabetes complications (two to three paragraphs).
3. Problems specifically related to the 'diabetic foot'.
4. Methods for diagnosing peripheral arterial disease. (All of the above provide background and context.)
5. Studies investigating biomarkers to diagnose peripheral arterial disease. This will be the crucial section, as it is here that you critically appraise the research done on the topic of interest and specifically clarify the gaps that still exist that you will address.

Use writing skills you have previously learned. Do a spell check, and have someone proofread your manuscript for flow and understanding. Ask someone who is not familiar with your work to proofread it for understanding and another to proofread for grammar.

Tips

- One idea per paragraph.
- Keep sentences short; cut long sentences up.
- Be brief and to the point.
- Write up in a manner that shows you are going to be a specialist in this area. Remember here who you are. You are a researcher, in control of your own destiny within your research. Be very critical of what you allow to influence the way you want to go forward in your research. Evaluate everything you read; take any good from it that will improve your study, and be circumspect about anything else. Justify in your review why you accept or reject any of the research you have read about.
- Check that your references are correctly formatted.

Pitfalls to avoid

- Do not merely create a list of who said what, with no evidence of your own intellectual input. This will not show how you have evaluated, assessed and synthesised the literature or applied other higher thinking skills.
- Do not write a long, rambling description of the concepts. Make sure the body of your review is subdivided into discrete sections, including headings where appropriate.

- Do not limit the depth and scope. You are required at your level of expertise to contribute to the body of knowledge of medical science. Make sure it is worthy, in terms of specificity and breadth.
- Do not write too much. For a protocol your review must be concise, show you are becoming an expert and fit into three to four pages.
- Do not include irrelevant literature. This will confuse and annoy readers.

Examples

Below are two examples of how the same literature can be cited in a paragraph from a literature review.

Example 1

Black et al (1998) have shown that XDR TB is resistant to at least four of the main therapies, while Brown (1999) showed that there are resistance patterns to a further two. This was confirmed in a study by White (2001). However, Green (2002) stated that it is not possible to come to any conclusions concerning …

Example 2

There have been several investigations that have shown that XDR TB has resistance patterns to … (Black et al, 1998; Brown, 1999; White, 2001). Green (2002) however, states that it is not possible to come to any conclusions

The first example cites the literature as a mere shopping list of studies, while the second shows that the writer has been able to synthesise and evaluate the literature.

Exercise

Search for a recent journal article that would be relevant to you. The article's introduction should include a concise literature review. Having read the above do's and don'ts, look at the piece critically and write down what the strengths and the weaknesses of the review are.

Conducting the literature review

Literature review checklist

Once you have written up your literature review, run through the following checklist. If you cannot answer 'yes' to every question, review your writing until you can. Only then should you send it to your supervisor for checking.

- Is the context for your study clearly stated?
- Is your review written so that your critical view is clearly evident?
- Does it start with the broad literature review and then narrow down to the specific area where your research idea is embedded?
- Have you clearly delineated aspects of your argument with subheadings?
- Is the review focused and relevant? For example, is it free of superfluous information?
- Is a clear picture of existing knowledge given?
- Is it clear where there is a gap in the literature?
- Is the need for your study well justified?
- Is your writing clear and free of confusing language?
- Are the references perfectly formatted within the requested referencing style?

Learning points

To justify and inform your study, you have to go to the literature to see what the state of research is in your particular area of interest. You need to read broadly as well as in depth, and glean information that is specifically important to your own study. You need to represent what you have learned from your reading in a literature review, and you have to acknowledge those sources you quote from, or refer to, in your text, as well as in the list of references, in a very particular style, which must be adhered to without exception.

Selecting an appropriate study design

An optimal study design is one that is best for the study purposes in terms of achieving the objectives, while being both time- and cost-efficient and within the scope of the research. Each design has advantages and disadvantages. The main steps to selecting your optimum study design involve asking the following questions:

- Is your study *observational* or *interventional*? Observational studies do not involve intervention or experimental manipulation.
- If observational, is it *descriptive* or *analytical*? Descriptive studies do not test any specific hypotheses. In analytical studies, the objective is usually to determine if there is an association between the independent variable/risk factor and the outcome. Thus, you will require a group with, and a group without, the outcome. For example, in a study to assess whether gender is associated with metabolic syndrome, a group with, and a group without, metabolic syndrome is required in order to compare the gender distribution in both groups and conclude whether there is, or is not, an association.
- Are you assessing *prevalence* or *incidence* of the outcome? Prevalence measures the burden of disease in a population at one point in time; incidence measures new cases over time.

A note on descriptive studies

What is the role of descriptive studies? The first phase of a research enquiry is often just to describe the existing situation in order to uncover problems that exist. These problems could then be investigated further through analytical research. Too seldom, however, do departments move beyond the descriptive phase. There should be structures in place so that every descriptive study is followed up by an analytical or intervention study.

Many students are tempted to do just a simple descriptive study. Always try to rather have a hypothesis that requires an analytical study. For example, rather than just describing the proportion of medical students who smoke, test the hypothesis that female students (or males) are more likely to be smokers; or, even better, test the provocative hypothesis that smokers on average have higher marks than non-smokers.

selecting an appropriate study design

> You will get the description of the percentage of male or female smokers anyway and you would have a far more interesting study that answers a particular question.

Types of study design

There are several study designs available. Look at your study carefully and decide which one will fit best. Here are some examples:

- *Cross-sectional study*: Participants are evaluated at one point in time (subjects can be recruited prospectively and are not all seen on the same day).
- *Cohort study*: Start with exposure status. Participants are classified as exposed and non-exposed (smokers, non-smokers). Cases (stroke) are identified over time, backwards in time (retrospective) or forwards in time (prospective), and the risk of outcome is compared between exposed and non-exposed.
- *Randomised clinical trial*: This is similar to a cohort study, except that the exposure (therapy) is assigned randomly.
- *Case-control study*: Start with cases. Select cases (subjects with hepatoma) preferably as they happen (new incident cases) and evaluate their exposure status. Select controls (subjects without the outcome), evaluate their exposure status and compare between cases and controls.

The following decision tree will guide your decision about what kind of study would be best for your research objectives.

1. **Observational study**
    1.1 **Descriptive objective**
        1.1.1 Prevalence — *cross-sectional study/survey*
            Example: To assess the prevalence of smoking in high school learners
        1.1.2 Incidence — *prospective/retrospective cohort study*
            Example: To measure the incidence of TB in HIV-positive patients during their first year of HAART
        1.1.3 KAPB (knowledge, attitudes, practices and beliefs) — *cross-sectional survey*
            Example: To describe the knowledge and attitudes of general practitioners towards health legislation
        1.1.4 Audit/review — *'retrospective' record review*
            Example: To audit the outcomes of a PMTCT programme
    1.2 **Analytical objective**: To show an association between a risk factor and an outcome

1.2.1 Prevalence
　1.2.1.1 Is the outcome rare? A group of cases in a hospital if the outcome is rare — *case-control study*
　Example: A group of lung cancer cases could be more easily accessed from a hospital ward than in the community.
　1.2.1.2 Is the outcome fairly common? Survey of population — *cross-sectional study*
　Example: A study on lower back pain could be carried out as a survey since lower back pain is relatively common and easy to identify.
1.2.2 Incidence: New cases of the outcome over time — *cohort study*
　Example: To examine the effect of antipsychotic drugs on the incidence of newly diagnosed cases of metabolic syndrome over a period of time

2. ***Interventional/experimental study*** (the researcher introduces an intervention)
　2.1 Randomised controlled trial
　　2.1.1 Individually randomised trial
　　Example: The effect of vitamin D supplementation on TB cure rate
　　2.1.2 Community or cluster randomised trial
　　Example: The effect of an educational HIV/AIDS preventive strategy in high schools

Pitfalls to avoid

- The purpose and scope of your study will determine the design, not the other way around. Do not try to choose a design first and then adapt your purpose and scope around the design.
- Many novice researchers try to design an analytical study without including a *comparison group*. For example, a researcher wanted to determine if HIV is a risk factor for pre-eclampsia in pregnant women. The proposed methodology entailed a record review of the HIV status of all pre-eclampsia cases at a particular hospital in 2009. Using this design, the researcher would not have been able to test if HIV is associated with pre-eclampsia because there is no non-pre-eclamptic group with which to compare the HIV status.
- Bear in mind that not all studies have to be analytical. Sometimes, very valuable information can be gained from studies that are purely descriptive.

A note on clinical trials

Some students may want to do a (small) *randomised controlled clinical trial* to test the efficacy of an intervention. You must ensure that your protocol adheres

Selecting an appropriate study design

to the criteria set out by the Consort Statement (www.consort-statement.org/) for publication of trials. (However, you can only comply with these if you were aware of them at the study design/protocol stage.) Also note that the randomisation of a small number of subjects is highly unlikely to balance prognostic factors between groups, and other methods such as minimisation or matching should be considered instead of randomisation.

In certain instances, clinics are randomised instead of individual patients (cluster randomised trials), and these require specialist input at the protocol stage. (You need input from someone experienced in clinical trial protocols for any clinical trial!)

Note that intervention studies have to be registered with the NHREC's online ethics application system (www.ethicsapp.co.za) as well as at www.clinicaltrials.gov.

Similarly, diagnostic studies should comply with certain validity criteria. The STARD Statement provides guidelines (www.stard-statement.org/). Similar to drug studies (Phase 1–4), diagnostic studies can also be done in phases and the study designs can vary.

Exercise

A student proposes to undertake a cancer screening study, with the following objectives.

The primary objectives are:

1. to determine if new method B, using a ……………, can be used as an alternative screening modality instead of the standard method A, in patients screened for carcinoma X; and
2. to assess the distribution of virus Y in the healthy population and in patients with carcinoma X.

The secondary objective is:

- to assess the incidence of carcinoma X in the population and in people with high titres of virus Y.

The research statement drives the study design, which in turn determines the format the analysis will take. In the above example, which study design should the student specify in the protocol? Write your answer in the space provided below.

_____

_____

_____
_____
_____

Answer

For the primary objectives:

1. This will require a cross-sectional comparative diagnostic study, requiring prospective screening of patients with both methods. If both methods are screening tools only, then the patients also need to have diagnosis verified by a gold standard. For various diagnostic study options, see Pencina MJ, D'Agostino RB, Vasan RS. Statistical methods for assessment of added usefulness of new biomarkers. *Clinical Chemistry and Laboratory Medicine* 2010;48(12):1703–11.
2. This will require a cross-sectional study of viral serology frequency.

For the secondary objective:

1. This will require a prospective cohort study for incidence to be calculated.

So it is clear that, in order to meet all objectives, what will be required is a prospective cohort study with a cross-sectional evaluation at baseline (all analytical studies such as cohort studies, case-control studies and clinical trials provide cross-sectional descriptive information at baseline).

Exercise

Name your main study objective and then choose the optimum study design. Give reasons why you chose that design.

Main study objective:

_____
_____
_____
_____

Selecting an appropriate study design

Optimum study design (select one):

- The study will be a prospective cohort study.
- The study will be a cross-sectional study.
- The study will be a cross-sectional diagnostic study.
- The study will be a cross-sectional comparative study of two groups.
- The study will be a case-control study.
- The study will be a controlled trial.

Reasons for your choice:

_____
_____
_____
_____

Study design checklist

Is the study design appropriate for the research objective(s)?

Learning points

The study design you adopt should be informed by your research objectives. You need to be able to discern whether your study is observational or interventional, descriptive or analytical, or whether you are looking at prevalence or incidence. Once you have clarity on this, you can decide which of the following study designs best fits your purpose: cross-sectional, cohort, randomised clinical trial or a case-control study.

Measurement

The final research report has to be *relevant* (answer an important question), *valid* (be free of bias), *accurate* (provide a result as close to the truth as possible), *repeatable or precise* (repeatable within a narrow range of possible answers) and *sufficiently powered* (in order to avoid a false negative result) to detect an effect size (difference between groups, for example) should a clinically meaningful one exist.

In this section you are going to define the *measurements* used to collect data on the demographics, important descriptors, exposure and outcome variables. This means you have to define which variables you are going to use (to describe your population, the exposure or the outcome, if relevant).

The measurement tools required are determined by the research statement and the study design, and vary from instruments such as Baumanometers and laboratory equipment to questionnaires.

Examples

- *Prevalence study of smoking habits amongst medical students*: How are you going to measure smoking status? Will you just ask: 'Do you smoke?', or are you also interested in type of tobacco, number of cigarettes etc? Is there a validated questionnaire used in other studies with settings and populations similar to yours?
- *Case-control study of hepatoma and oral contraceptive use*: How are the cases detected and diagnosed? How and where are the controls selected? How is oral contraceptive use measured (similar issues in as above example)?
- *Randomised controlled trial of drugs that lower blood pressure*: How, and how often, is the blood pressure measured, with which instrument (approved by the relevant bodies such as the Southern African Hypertension Society) and which method (validated, guideline-driven)?

Important terminology

- **Accuracy:** This means getting a result as close to the truth as possible (hitting the bull's-eye on the target).

② *Precision:* This means repeatability. If you take six samples from one patient, they should all give a very similar result.

③ *Measurement error:* There are two components to measurement error: random error and systematic error (bias). Random error is the error expected just by chance. Random error is unpredictable. With systematic error, the direction and/or magnitude of error are not just random (for example, the Baumanometer overestimates the systolic blood pressure by 5 mm Hg on all subjects). Various forms of error can contribute to variation in results; examples are instrument or laboratory variability, subject variability (cortisol values vary depending on time of day) and observer variability (when more than one observer does blood pressure or ultrasound measurements, they may vary). To avoid the latter, observers should be kept to a minimum, training should be done according to a standardised protocol, and testing of inter- and intra-observer variability (to show that it is minimal prior to commencing the study) should be done.

Adequate training, pre-study practice, pilot studies, standardised manuals of operation, calibration of instruments and double data entry are all ways to minimise random and systematic error. For more information on measurement error, see www.socialresearchmethods.net/kb/measerr.php.

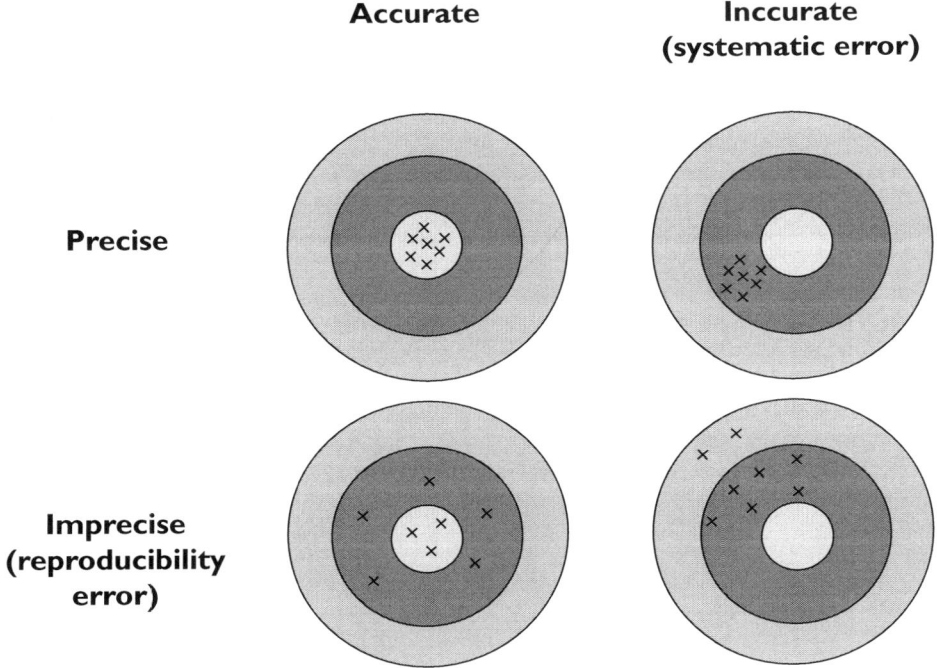

Figure 1: The components of error
Source: www.wellesley.edu/Chemistry/Chem105manual/Appendices/uncertainty_analysis.html

Validity: This means that your results are free from bias. Essentially, there are three forms of bias:

1. *Selection bias:* For example, volunteers are used to test a new exercise programme. Volunteers tend to be more health-conscious, younger and healthier.
2. *Information bias:* For example, patients are seen four times weekly in one arm of a trial and six times weekly in the other. Another example is recall bias, where mothers of sick children are more likely to recall drug exposure than mothers of healthy controls.
3. *Confounding bias:* For example, you show an association between alcohol use and lip cancer. The association, however, is confounded by smoking (people who drink a lot also tend to be smokers) and the true cause is smoking and not alcohol.

Your protocol should not only address the measurements used in the study but ideally should also mention what you will do to ensure validity, accuracy and precision. This is done in a measurement statement.

Example of a measurement statement in the protocol

Stored blood from the 1992 study clinic visit, which we considered the baseline for all present analyses, is available for fatty acid measurements. Blood was drawn after 12 hours of fasting, stored at –70 °C, and shipped on dry ice for centralised long-term storage at –80 °C.

Fatty acid measurements will be performed at the Hudson Cancer Research Center, which will provide quantitative measurement of 45 fatty acids as a percentage of total fatty acids.

Total lipids will be extracted from plasma by using the methods of .... and colleagues (reference), and phospholipids will be separated from neutral lipids by using one-dimensional, thin-layer chromatography. Samples of fatty acid methyl ester will be prepared by direct transesterification by using the methods of .... and .... (reference) and separated by using gas chromatography (5890 gas chromatograph flame ionisation detector, Agilent Technologies, Palo Alto, California; SP-2560 fused-silica 100-m capillary column, Supelco, Belefonte, Pennsylvania; initial, 160 °C × 16 min; ramp, 3.0 °C/min to 240 °C; hold, 15 min).

Adapted from Mozaffarian D, Cao H, King IB, Lemaitre RN, Song X, Siscovick DS & Hotamisligil GS. Trans-palmitoleic acid, metabolic risk factors, and new-onset diabetes in U.S. adults: a cohort study. *Annals of Internal Medicine* 2010 Dec 21;153(12):790–9.

Exercise

Now write down your section on measurement.

Learning points

In terms of <u>measuring your data,</u> you need to be aware of <u>relevance, validity, accuracy, repeatability, power and bias</u>. These need to be addressed early on in defining your variables within your <u>study design and showing what you intend to measure in the form of a measurement statement</u>.

Research participant selection

It is important to understand and define the concepts of the *theoretical population, study population, sampling frame* and *sample population*.

Who do you want to generalise to?

Answer: The theoretical population

This refers to those to whom you would like the results of the study to be generalisable (for example, all elderly patients with hypertension).

Which subjects can you get access to?

Answer: The study population

If you cannot study the entire study population, you can take a sample of the population. The sample must be *representative of the study population* and of *sufficient size*.
   Study populations must be defined in terms of:

- *person (who):* for example, persons over 60 years diagnosed with stroke;
- *place (where):* for example, eThekwini municipality; and
- *time (when):* only when appropriate (for example, elderly patients seen at primary care clinics).

How can you get access to them?

Answer: The sampling frame (for example, clinic registers)

Who is in your study?

Answer: The sample

For more information on sampling terminology, see www.socialresearchmethods.net/kb/sampterm.php.
   You now need to define your theoretical population, your study population, your sampling frame and your sample. These need to be defined because they precede important issues such as *sampling methods* and *inclusion and exclusion criteria*.

Research participant selection

> *Exercise*
>
> Who is your theoretical population? _____
>
> Who is your study population? _____

Sampling strategies

To ensure that your sample is representative of the population, you can limit bias by using *probability sampling*. This means ensuring that all members of the population have an equal probability of being selected for the sample.

- *Simple random sampling*, if possible, is the most desirable strategy. In many situations it is not possible; for example, in a study to assess the health status of older persons in a community, a simple random sample might not be possible due to the sampling frame (a list of all population units) not being available. Even if such a list were available and we could take a random sample from it, it might not be possible to reach all the selected individuals due to the size of the population or their exact locations being unknown.
- *Stratified sampling* should be used if you need to ensure proportional representation from each stratum. For example, first stratify the population into males and females and then take a random sample from each stratum using probability proportional to size sampling.
- *Cluster sampling* should be used if you have a large geographic area to sample and individuals are found within many clusters.
    - First take a random sample of clusters (for example, hospitals or schools), and then take a sample of individuals from within the selected clusters.
    - Try to avoid this method of sampling, if possible, since the sample size determination and analysis is really tricky.
- *Systematic sampling*: every *Nth* record is selected from a list, or every *Nth* house chosen on a street.
- For record reviews or studies that require a sample of patients attending a doctor's practice or hospital, a *consecutive sample* of patients meeting inclusion criteria who present between two defined dates can be taken if it can be assumed that the order in which patients present is random.

Writing your first clinical research protocol

Exercise

What type of sampling method is most appropriate for your study? Tick your choice and provide a rationale.

Simple random sampling _____

Stratified sampling _____

Cluster sampling _____

Systematic sampling _____

Consecutive sampling _____

Note: Most statistical tests assume that simple random sampling has taken place.

Sample size

What is a sufficient size for a sample? There is no magic one-size-fits-all answer. Each study needs to be considered individually. In reality, sample size is usually limited by logistical constraints, such as:

- cost;
- time; and
- availability of participants.

Now consider your own study

1. First consider how many participants your budget and time constraints will allow (logistical sample size).
   Write your answer here: _____
2. Now use sample size software like Epi Info™ (www.cdc.gov/epiinfo/) or the calculators on www.openepi.com/OE2.3/menu/openEpiMenu.htm or sampsize.sourceforge.net/iface/index.html to help you determine the optimum statistical sample size for your study.

   Write your answer here: _____
3. Ideally, use the optimal statistical sample size if it is smaller than the logistical sample size. In reality, however, the optimal sample size is often larger than the logistical sample size, so alternative strategies need to be considered. For example, say there are only four patients meeting inclusion criteria per week coming to a clinic in your sampling area. You have only a month to collect data and 16 patients will not provide you with sufficient power for your study.

Research participant selection

> You could consider including another clinic in your sample and expanding your population's geographical location, if applicable. Alternatively, you could change the scope of your study to a pilot study, which would be more exploratory in nature and not test any hypotheses. However, the strategy you use should suit the purposes of your research.

Essential information you will need in order to calculate the optimum statistical sample size

Consider your main objective for the study. This will be the objective from which your sample size is calculated. Write it down in the space provided below:

_____

_____

Is it descriptive or analytical? _____

If descriptive: Here you are not testing a hypothesis, so sufficient power to find a difference, should it exist, is not the issue; the issue is, with what level of precision do you want to report your results? (How wide do you want your confidence interval to be?)

- What is the approximate population size?
- What is the estimated prevalence of the factor under study in the population?
- How precise would you like your sample to be? For example, a researcher aims to estimate the prevalence of dementia in persons aged 60 years and above in TAFTA residential homes in inner Durban. There is a total of 1 371 persons in this defined population, and the population prevalence is thought to be 20%. The researcher wants the sample estimate to be within 4% of the population value; thus the required sample size at 95% confidence is 300.
- Level of confidence (usually 95%)

If analytical:

- Cross-sectional/randomised controlled trial/cohort study:
    - What is the ratio of exposed to unexposed participants?
    - What is the expected prevalence/incidence of the outcome in those with, and without, the exposure?
- Comparing means between two groups:
    - What is the difference between the means that will be clinically important to detect?
    - What is the standard deviation of the measurement (as expected in group 1 and group 2)? For example, a researcher is comparing two

groups (intervention and control) with blood pressure as the outcome. The investigators determined that a 5 mm Hg difference between groups would be clinically important to detect. It is known from the literature that the standard deviation of systolic blood pressure is 15 mm Hg. To have 80% power to detect a difference of 5 mm Hg as significant (given a sd of 15) you will need 142 subjects per group.

- Case-control study:
  - What is the ratio of cases to controls?
  - What is the expected prevalence of the exposure in cases and in controls?
- Level of significance (usually 95%)
- Power required (at least 80%). For example, a researcher hypothesises that ethnicity is associated with fractures in post-menopausal women. The researcher conducts an analytical cross-sectional study to compare the prevalence of fractures in African and Indian women. Sample size calculation was based on the assumption of a 56% prevalence of fractures in African women and 29% prevalence in Indian women, as well as a 1:2 ratio of African to Indian women attending the clinic where the research is being carried out. These estimates were obtained in a pilot study. Sample sizes of 43 Africans and 82 Indians achieve 80% power to detect a difference between the group proportions of 27%, with 95% confidence.

Some rules of thumb:

- To detect one standard deviation difference between two groups (15 mm Hg in the above example) you would need 16 subjects per group (80% power).
- To detect a half standard deviation difference between two groups (80% power) you would need 64 subjects per group.
- Note that the larger the difference you want to detect, the smaller the sample size.
- The larger the standard deviation, the larger the sample size needed.

Other factors to consider:

- Loss of research participants over time in follow-up studies (where the design is longitudinal). This can occur due to death, migration or participant drop-out.
- Controlling for confounders will require a larger sample size.
- Planned subgroup analyses.
- If you are using a cluster sample, you need to adjust your sample size by the design factor, which is a measure of how correlated respondents are expected to be within a cluster.

The information you need usually comes from previously published or unpublished studies similar to yours on similar populations. If there aren't any, or if those which are available are not generalisable to your population, you need to use a best educated guess (or that of your supervisor or an expert in the field).

Finally, see a statistician to confirm your sample size only when you have gathered as much as possible of the above information. Most importantly, you need to have a difference or effect in mind that will be clinically meaningful to detect. This is a clinical decision, not a statistical one, but is crucial for determining the correct sample size.

> ### Learning points
>
> In order for your research to be seen as credible by the rest of the scientific community, you need to define precisely who your research participants are. In addition, for your results to be considered statistically significant, you need to find out exactly how many participants you will need in your study.

Ethics and ethical approval

In the protocol, your data analysis and *ethics* sections typically follow after all the other issues, such as objectives, literature review and methods, have been dealt with. It is crucial, however, that you consider the ethical implications of your research *prior* to writing your research proposal.

The *ethical requirements* vary depending on whether the research is primarily laboratory-based or whether it involves human or animal subjects. Basically every study involving medical research has ethical implications. Participants are selected, questioned, examined, tested and given exposures such as drugs or exercise, creating different scenarios which require ethical reasoning on the part of the investigator.

Obtaining *informed consent* (or getting the required authorisation when informed consent is not needed or unavailable) is a primary requisite for most medical research projects. The informed consent document needs to be added as an appendix to the protocol. Most institutions require this document to be in a particular format, depending on the type of study conducted. You will need to contact your institution's research or ethics office for examples. This document should be written in a manner that will be understandable to a layperson with primary school education. Examples and templates exist depending on the type of study, and you should obtain these from your local *ethics committee*.

Other important principles

1. *Value:* Does this research generate or enhance our current knowledge base?
2. *Scientific validity:* The methodology must address and avoid bias and be scientifically rigorous.
3. *Fair subject selection:* Inclusion and exclusion criteria should be driven by clear scientific objectives and not by vulnerability or privilege.
4. *Favourable risk–benefit ratio:* Within the context of standard clinical practice and the research protocol, risks must be minimised and potential benefits enhanced, keeping in mind that the potential benefits need to outweigh the risks for individuals or communities.
5. *Independent review:* Usually this means that an independent ethics review committee approves, and can amend or terminate, a study.
6. *Respect for enrolled subjects:* This includes ensuring privacy and confidentiality of information, for example.

Sometimes institutions require the protocol to be reviewed by an appropriate *academic committee* prior to ethics committee submission. This is to ensure that the first two principles are adhered to. When submitting to the ethics committee, ensure that you carefully follow the instructions for submission of your protocol. Often, the protocol has to be submitted a month or more in advance, and submitting an incomplete set of documents could delay your application.

If you plan to do any intervention study (such as a clinical trial), most ethics committees will require you to have completed a training course in Good Clinical Practice (GCP). This is to ensure that the investigator adheres to sound ethical, scientific and management practices when doing research on human subjects.

If there are children younger than seven years in your study, the parents must give consent on their behalf; for children between 7 and 18 years, parents must give consent for their child to participate in the study and the child must also give assent.

Take note that if your research involves animals you will have to obtain approval from your institution's ethics committee for research on animals.

Example of an ethics section in the protocol

All patients who volunteer to participate will be asked to provide written informed consent as a prerequisite for inclusion. The study will commence only after it has been approved by the University of .... Ethics Committee. Patient data will be entered into a database, with each patient allocated a study number. No patient identifiers, such as address etc, will be entered. The risk of the study is negligible, since only a questionnaire is used and no interventions are done. Principles of Helsinki and Good Clinical Practice will be adhered to. The informed consent document can be found as Appendix 1.

Exercise

List the requirements your institution has for the submission of a protocol for ethics approval. Use this list as a checklist when compiling your submission.

_____

_____

_____

_____

Writing your first clinical research protocol

> *Learning points*
>
> In order to ensure that all research participants are protected within your research paradigm, you have to acquire ethical approval from an ethics committee. Your application for ethics approval must be accurately compiled, and all information and signatures requested must be supplied.

The data collection instrument

When <u>collecting data</u> from various sources, you need to design an instrument that will ensure that the same data is collected from every data source, be it a study participant or a patient record. These instruments generally take the form of either a *questionnaire* or a *data extraction form*.

The instrument should be both <u>valid and reliable</u>. It is easiest to use an already <u>validated instrument if you can get permission from the original author</u>. However, you may find that your study design requires a <u>uniquely designed instrument</u>, in which case you must bear the following points in mind:

- *Layout*
  - Consider whether the instrument will be self-administered or not. If it is to be self-administered, use basic vocabulary and concise, clear and unambiguous questions. Include instructions on how each question should be answered; for example, 'tick all that apply', 'select the most appropriate response' etc.
  - Use tick boxes and closed-ended questions rather than open-ended questions.
  - The instrument must not be too long. People lose patience and focus if they are expected to spend too much time on a questionnaire.
- *Questions*
  - Make sure <u>confidentiality</u> is maintained.
  - <u>Match questions explicitly to your aims or research statement.</u>
  - Keep the scale of measurement in mind (see key concept 1 in the section on preparing your plan for data analysis) and consider how you plan to analyse each variable (also in aforementioned section).
  - Your instrument should be <u>mutually exclusive</u> and <u>exhaustive</u>.
  - Make sure the wording of questions is <u>non-contradictory</u>.
  - Questions should not be <u>leading</u>.
  - Ask only <u>one question at a time</u>.
  - Arrange questions in a <u>logical and coherent order</u>.
  - Include an option for '<u>missing/don't know</u>' responses.
- *Validity and reliability:* A <u>valid question is one that tests what is supposed to be tested. A reliable question is one that will produce similar results on different occasions under constant conditions. In order to collect data that are both reliable and valid, the questions should be critically assessed. The reviewing of probes by colleagues can be used to ensure that a degree of validity was</u>

Writing your first clinical research protocol

attained. This type of validity is termed face validity. Pilot your questionnaire to test face validity and feasibility.

Tips for analysis and coding

- Variables which can be collected as quantitative should be: for example, age should not be categorised on the data collection form. You can always categorise it later if you need to, and you can get much more information from the quantitative variable such as mean, standard deviation and range.
- Categorical variables should be coded on the original questionnaire.
- Multiple-response fields require separate fields for each possible response; for example, 'symptoms: shortness of breath, wheezing, tight chest, coughing'. Try to limit multiple-response fields in favour of mutually exclusive variables for ease of analysis.

Learning points

A questionnaire is an important tool to collect the same data consistently from each research participant. Care should be taken in the design of the instrument to ensure that all the information for all the variables can be adequately recorded.

Limitations of the research

What are study limitations?

No study can ever yield results that can be generalised to explain the same research statements in every situation. The results you obtain on your study strictly explain the problem for that particular study group only. Using common sense, we generally use the explanation for the results and infer that the results could be the same if the experiment were to be repeated elsewhere. But we cannot do this with absolute certainty. Different contexts can deliver very different results for the same study. You should qualify your conclusions from your results by stating where the results will hold and where they will not hold. Every study has delimitations that define the scope of the study and limitations that set boundaries to the inferences you may make from the data.

There are some instances where variables in the study are fixed, and these variables could be different in another sample. These are variables that are often not considered in the study design because they are irrelevant in the context. For example, one could be studying lactic acidosis in patients on HAART in rural Zululand and come up with findings that are important in ARV therapy for that particular group. But the same study in Johannesburg, conducted on a diverse group of cultures, could yield very different results. It may be that the population that you are studying have a high incidence of a mutation within the mitochondrial genome which results in lactic acidosis in patients receiving ARVs.

It is important to establish the limitations of the research in the early stages of designing the research proposal, for two reasons:

1. This exercise will define the parameters of the research for the study.
2. Any adjustments to the research design which could ameliorate the limitations should be made early on in the research design process.

Some intrinsic limitations to studies

There are some study designs that have intrinsic limitations:

- *Case studies* are descriptive in nature and include data from only one or very few individuals. In most instances, case studies are published because they are anomalies, and not typical. The results of case studies cannot be generalised to the entire population.

- *Correlation studies* demonstrate that one variable can be predicted from another variable. In the study, you may be seeking a causal relationship between the variables. However, alternative explanations for correlational findings could also exist. The correlation found may only hold among certain groups, under specific conditions, or there could be a third variable that causes the two variables without there actually being a relationship between the first two variables.
- In *randomised experiments*, the specificity of the groups selected, as well as their context, could preclude results from being generalisable.

Exercise

1. Name the limitations of your research in terms of the group you have selected to study as well as the environment in which the study will take place. (Hint: look at the scope of your study.)

   _____
   _____
   _____
   _____

2. What time and financial constraints are there on the study?

   _____
   _____
   _____

3. Formulate a statement setting out the limitations of your study and indicating how you will address the above constraints.

   _____
   _____
   _____

Learning points

All research has its limitations. Some study designs have intrinsic limitations. There are also limitations specific to your study, such as time and budget, as well as complete generalisability.

Preparing your plan for data analysis

You will be required to provide some detail in your protocol on how you plan to analyse your data. The data analysis plan does not have to be cast in stone at this stage, unless you are conducting a clinical trial. It can usually evolve during the analysis phase of your study. However, the analysis planning stage is essential because it makes you think ahead and helps you ensure that your objectives are achievable using the type of data you plan to collect.

If you have no statistics training yet, you will need to attend a basic statistics course and have access to basic statistics textbooks or online resources. Once you have some basic competencies you will be able to carry out many of the tests yourself, but it is essential that you have your plan checked by a statistician, and have them run the more complex tests. Remember that you will need to interpret the results of the statistical analysis in order to write up your results and discussion sections. A statistician can guide you in this process, or collaborate with you in the study if your data requires more complex analysis.

Before you start planning your data analysis, it is important to be familiar with the key concepts described below.

Key concept 1: Scales of measurement

Variables are classified according to whether they are measured on a categorical scale (for example, HIV-positive or HIV-negative) or a numerical scale (for example, age of the patient).

Categorical variables are further classified as:

- *binary*: only two possible options; for example, employment — yes or no;
- *nominal*: more than two different groups, with no incremental order; for example, marital status — single, married, divorced or widowed; or
- *ordinal*: more than two different groups, with an incremental order; for example, severity of disease — mild, moderate, severe.

Numerical variables can be discrete (reflected as whole numbers only; for example, number of patients in a ward) or continuous (can be reflected as whole numbers and values between them; for example height). Figure 2 shows the organised breakdown of scales of measurement with more examples.

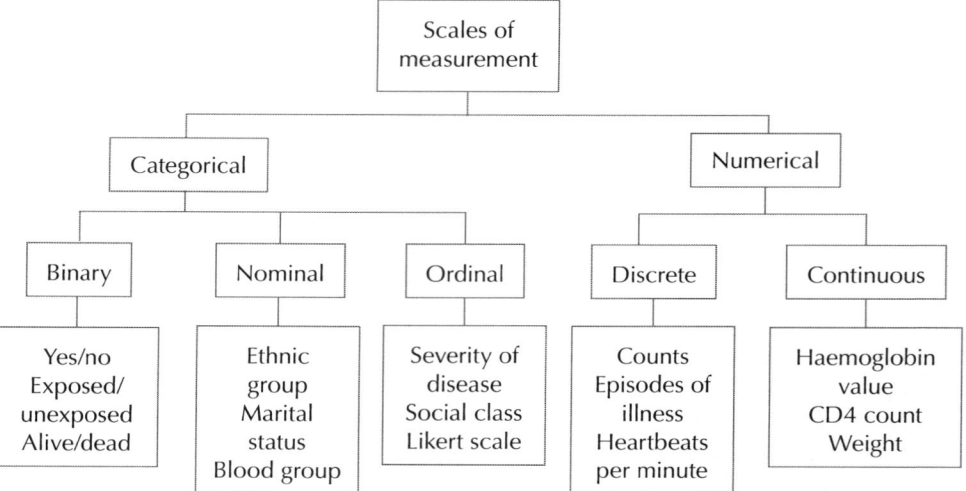

Figure 2: Scales of measurement

> ### Exercise
>
> What is the scale of measurement for the following types of data?
> 1. IQ score _____
> 2. Housing type _____
> 3. Movie ratings _____
> 4. Monthly income _____
> 5. Distance _____
> 6. Cholesterol level _____
> 7. Parity _____
> 8. Answer to the question: 'Have you experienced post-traumatic stress disorder after the hijacking?' _____

Key concept 2: Normal or non-normal distributions

Numerical variables that have a bell-shaped, symmetrical probability distribution, which is evenly distributed around the mean value, are said to be normally distributed. When outlying high or low values skew the curve, the distribution is said to be non-normal.

The histogram in Figure 3 shows the distribution of haemoglobin values in HIV-positive patients starting ARV treatment. The distribution is relatively normal since the majority of values are around the middle of the distribution and there are few very high or very low values.

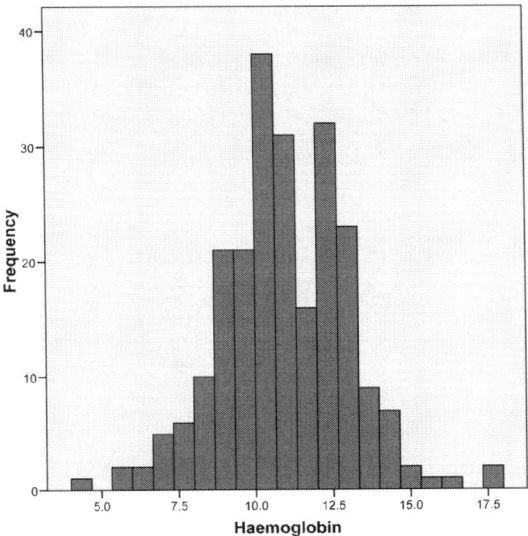

Figure 3: An example of a normal distribution

The histogram in Figure 4 shows the distribution of CD4 cell counts in the same group of patients. Here the disribution is non-normal, as the majority have low values and there are very few with high values; thus the mean will be skewed towards the low values.

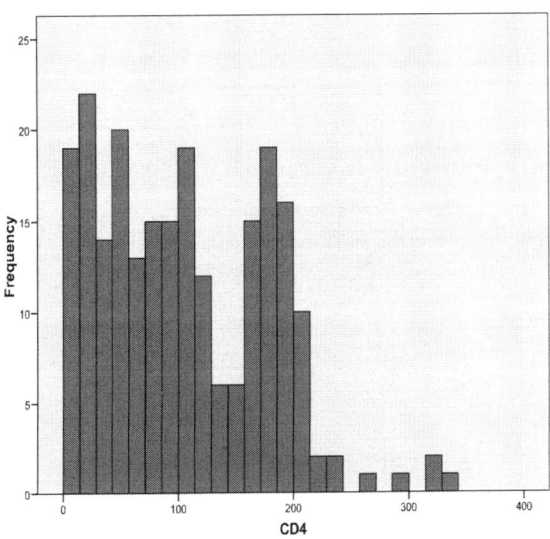

Figure 4: An example of a non-normal distribution

Key concept 3: Independent and paired groups

Whether you are using a matched (paired) design or an independent groups design will influence your choice of statistical tests. A paired design eliminates much of the variability normally found between subjects, and thus leads to smaller standard errors and more significant results. However, using analysis intended for paired designs on independent data, and vice versa, will lead to invalid results. Use Figure 5 to help you decide whether your design is paired, independent or has elements of both designs.

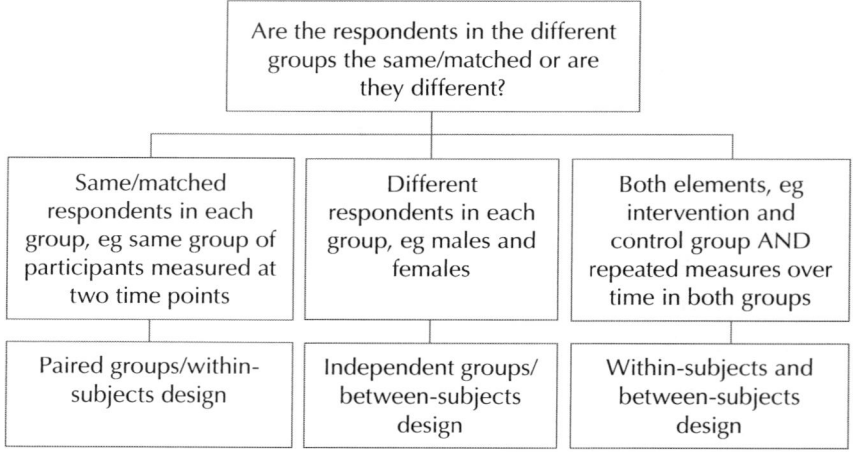

Figure 5: Independent and paired groups research designs

Key concept 4: Independent and dependent variables

Usually, epidemiological research seeks to show an association between an exposure and an outcome.

- The dependent variable (DV) is the outcome or response variable.
- The independent variable (IV) is the exposure or risk factor.
- Confounders are associated with the IV, and are independent risk factors for the DV.

For example, a researcher hypothesises that HIV infection of mothers (IV) is a risk factor for preterm delivery of infants (DV), but the presence of pre-eclampsia (confounder) also needs to be taken into account since it might be associated with HIV infection and an independent risk factor for preterm delivery.

Preparing your plan for data analysis

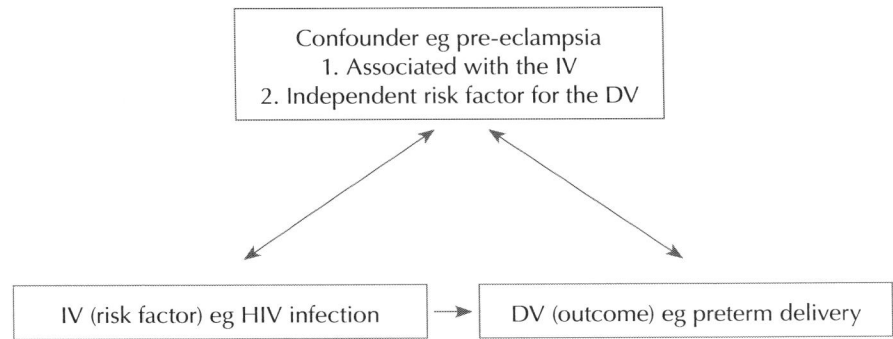

Figure 6: An example of the effect of confounding in the association between an independent variable and a dependent variable

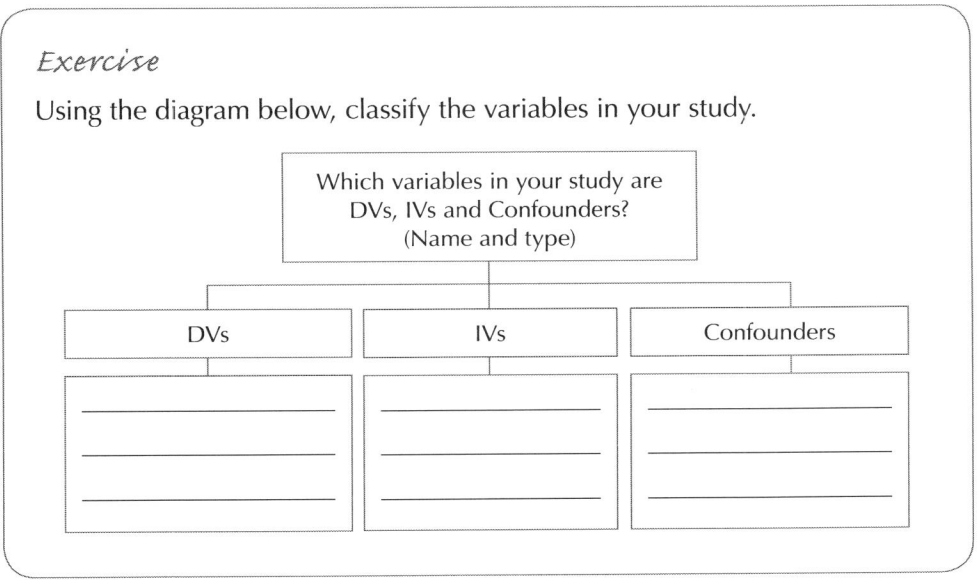

How do you select the appropriate statistical test for your variables?

The following dichotomous key (Table 1) and the algorithm which follows it (Figure 7) can be used as a guide to choosing the most appropriate statistical test or procedure to include in the statistical planning section of your protocol. It is not all-inclusive, and advice from a statistician should be sought to confirm your statistical plan. Furthermore, the key is only applicable for univariate and bivariate analysis; thus, if adjustment for confounders is required, more complex statistical models are often needed.

Writing your first clinical research protocol

In a dichotomous key, you make a choice between two options and then you are guided to the next point where you will make yet another choice between two options. So in the dichotomous key below, you are asked to make a choice between testing a hypothesis in your study or not. If you are testing a hypothesis, you go to point 4, where you are asked to make a choice between whether or not you are comparing groups in your study. If you are comparing groups in your study, you will go to point 7, where you are asked whether your groups are paired or independent. And so you go on until you get to the final suggestion for your test.

Table 1: Dichotomous key for statistical test selection

Choice option	Choice	Solution or next choice option
1	You are not testing a hypothesis	2
1	You are testing a hypothesis	4
2	The variable is categorical	frequency, relative frequency (%), confidence interval, bar chart
2	The variable is numerical	3
3	Normally distributed	mean, standard deviation, range confidence interval, error bar chart, histogram
3	Non-normally distributed	median, interquartile range, range, box and whisker plots
4	You are not comparing groups	5
4	You are comparing groups	7
5	You are not looking for relationships between quantitative variables	cluster analysis, factor analysis
5	You are looking for relationships between quantitative variables	6
6	Normally distributed	Pearson's correlation, linear regression
6	Non-normally distributed	Spearman's correlation
7	Groups are paired	8
7	Groups are independent	Go to Figure 7
8	There are two paired groups	9

Choice option	Choice	Solution or next choice option
8	There are more than two paired groups	12
9	Categorical dependent variable	10
9	Numerical dependent variable	11
10	Binary	McNemar's chi-square test
10	Ordinal	McNemar-Bowker chi-square test
11	Normally distributed	paired T-test
11	Non-normally distributed	Wilcoxon signed-ranks test
12	Categorical binary/counts dependent variable	Poisson regression, Generalised Linear Models for binomial family, Generalised Estimating Equations
12	Numerical dependent variable	13
13	Normally distributed	repeated measures ANOVA/ Generalised Linear Models
13	Non-normally distributed/ordinal	Friedman test, survival analysis

Now decide what types of variables the independent variable (IV) and the dependent variable (DV) are.

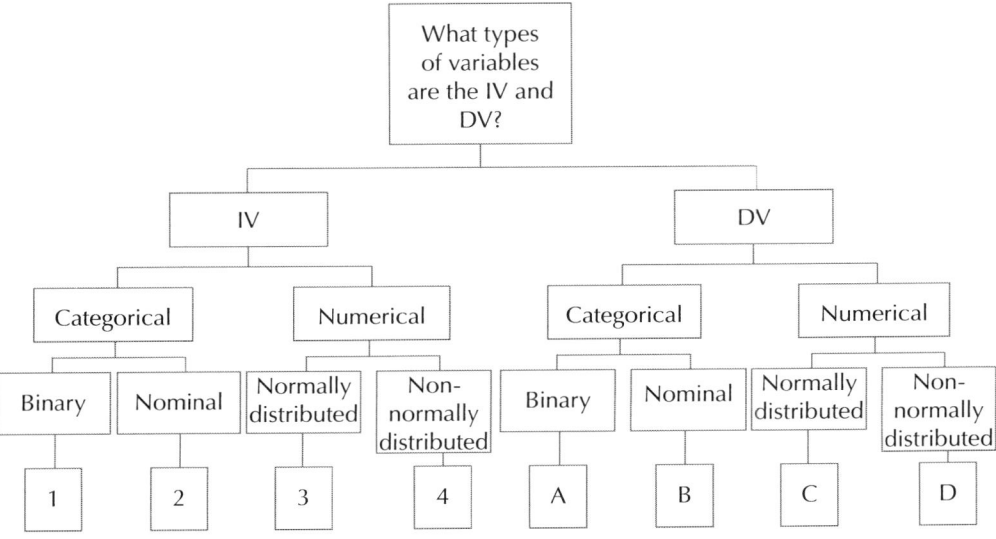

Figure 7: Algorithm for choice of statistical test for independent groups

Record the combination of 1–4 for the IV by A–D for the DV. (For example, if the IV is a non-normally distributed numerical value and the DV is a nominal categorical value, you will record 4B). Now choose a statistical test for your variables from the key below. (For the example here see 4B below; you will do a Kruskal-Wallis test.)

1A	Fisher's exact test or Pearson's chi-square test
1B	Pearson's chi-square test
1C	Independent samples T-test
1D	Mann-Whitney test
2A	Pearson's chi-square test
2B	Pearson's chi-square test
2C	ANOVA
2D	Kruskal-Wallis test
3A	Independent samples T-test
3B	ANOVA
3C	Pearson's correlation or linear regression
3D	Spearman's correlation
4A	Mann-Whitney test
4B	Kruskal-Wallis test
4C	Spearman's correlation
4D	Spearman's correlation

Example

In a study assessing whether participants' perceptions of their own weight was accurate, participants' weights in kilograms (a numerical, normally distributed dependent variable) were recorded, and they were then asked if they thought they were underweight, normal or overweight (nominal categorical independent variable). From the dichotomous key above, the path chosen is: 1, 4, 7, algorithm: 2C = ANOVA. Therefore the appropriate test to compare mean weight between the three categories of weight perception is ANOVA testing.

Exercise

Choose one IV and one DV from your list in the previous exercise. List the path chosen in the dichotomous key and algorithm above and state the name of the statistical test you arrive at:

_____

_____

Analysis of epidemiologic studies and clinical trials

When your interest is in comparing risk of disease between groups (for example, the risk of cancer in smokers versus non-smokers) a simple cross-tabulation with a chi-square test is not sufficient. In epidemiology there are *measures of disease frequency* (prevalence and incidence) as well as *measures of association* (relative risk and odds ratios). In a cohort study *relative risk* is calculated, whereas in a case-control study *odds ratios* are reported. Note that when logistic regression is used to determine association with a binary outcome (stroke versus no stroke, for example), the result is also reported as an odds ratio.

In clinical trials (and often in cohort studies), the outcome is not just whether an event occurs or not; the time to the outcome is more important. For this, survival analysis (typically with Cox proportional-hazards regression) is used and hazard ratios are reported.

Analysis of diagnostic studies

The analyses done depend on the aim and phase of the diagnostic research but generally require measures such as sensitivity, specificity, predictive values and likelihood ratios. For clinical prediction rules, logistic regression is often used. (See the references given in the section on study design, under diagnostic studies on page 27.)

Example of a data analysis and sample size section

The sample characteristics will be described with means, standard deviations and percentages (medians and ranges in the case of skewed data). The weight between the two groups will be compared with a Student T-test. The clinically significant difference we want to detect is 3 kg. To detect this difference (with a standard deviation of 4 kg from the literature) at alpha 0.05 and beta at 0.20 (80% power), given a weight of 80 kg in the standard group, we will need 28 subjects in each group. A P value of 0.05 is regarded as statistically significant.

Exercise

Write a paragraph on data analysis and sample size for your protocol.

Learning points

Different data types need to be treated differently when it comes to statistical analysis. It is important to be able to define the dependent and independent variables within a study, whether these are categorical or numerical, whether they have a normal or non-normal distribution, and whether the groups are paired or independent. Once this has been achieved, you can select an appropriate test.

Budgets and timelines

Most research protocols require you to mention whether funding for your project has been applied for, or has been received. Not all protocols require costs and timelines to be stipulated in detail, but it is a good idea to give this area some thought because it makes you think more deeply about the progress of your project.

Time and money both need to be budgeted right upfront in your study. By thinking about exactly what you will be doing, from the beginning of the project right through to the publication of the results, you will become aware of the investments that need to be made in order to achieve the results you anticipate from your research. Unbudgeted items can create a stumbling block that could seriously hamper your project's progress and threaten its completion. Underestimating or overestimating your budget could also affect the progress of your project. Underestimate, and you will not be able to complete the research; overestimate, and you will probably not get approval.

Budgets

Looking at your methods section, you will be able to allocate budget items to each step in your research process. All items required for the research to take place must be itemised, their needs justified and amounts allocated to them. Many online research application forms have templates for your budget items, which helps you by naming possible expense items. However, you may have to think it all out yourself; be very careful not to miss out any items.

There are several categories and subcategories of expenses that should be considered at each step of the research process. These include:

- *Staffing, subcontracting and consultation costs:* If you are not going to do all the work yourself, you will probably need to pay others to do some of it for you. You could be employing fieldworkers, nurses or translators. If you are sequencing genes, you may subcontract the sequencing to another organisation.
- *Supplies:* If your project has a laboratory component, you will have to cost in laboratory supplies. You may require specific equipment that you will need to buy for the project — a digital camera, for example, if you need photographic records of dysmorphologies. The costs of running several questionnaires through a photocopier must be accounted for somewhere.

- *Administration costs:* Sometimes your university research office will charge a percentage of a grant for administration costs. Your lab might charge bench fees per project, which you will have to account for in your budget. If you require specialist data analysis, this too must be costed into your budget.
- *Travel:* You, and possibly some of your fieldworkers, may need to do additional travelling in order to get to different data collection sites. In addition, you may want to travel to a conference after your project is complete in order to report on your study.
- *Patient costs:* Your study may involve some patient care costs that need to be covered. Also, you may decide to pay your study participants a small stipend to reimburse them for their travel costs should they come to your study site. You may also want to provide them with refreshments or other materials that will make their participation in the study worthwhile for them. There are very fine ethical lines here that have to be considered in order to ensure that the study participant does not take part in the research for the reimbursement, which is tantamount to coercion.
- *Publication and dissemination costs:* Sometimes you will need to pay an amount for your research paper to be published, especially if it is necessary to include colour pictures. If you are going to present your data anywhere, there will be costs involved, such as conference fees.

Very important to remember: If a study is to take place over a few years, costs may increase every year, and this increase will need to be factored into the original budget. If you use a spreadsheet, you can program a fixed annual increase into the total costing. Below is an example of a research budget for a study looking at finding two particular SNPs in patients experiencing hyperlactataemia when on HAART. The study was expected to be completed within a single year, with conference costs being allocated for the year after the completion of the study.

Table 2: Example of a research budget

Expense subcategories	Specific cost	Justification	2010 (Rands)	2011 (Rands)
Staffing	Consultant fees	A bioinformaticist will be consulted for this project.	10 000	
	Lab assistant costs	Laboratory technician required to do DNA isolations and PCRs.	30 000	
Subtotal			40 000	

Budgets and timelines

Materials and supplies	Blood draw kits	Needles and tubes required to draw blood from 50 patients and 50 volunteers	2 000	
	PCR costs	Costs of kits for two SNPs	80 000	
	Sequencing costs	The cost of two sequences from POLG for each participant	37 000	
	Contingency	Incidental costs, mainly due to price increases	10 000	
Subtotal			129 000	
Travel	International travel	Air travel to the USA for training/study visit	18 000	
	International subsistence	Principal investigator to spend six weeks in Dr Bill Hopeland's laboratory	36 000	
	Local conferences (travel and subsistence)	Two researchers to attend the South African Human Genetics Society Conference in 2011 to report findings of the study		20 000
Subtotal			54 000	20 000
Patient costs	Reimbursements	All participants will be given R50 to cover the costs of the visit to the clinic for the blood draw. This will cover transport and meal costs.	5 000	
Subtotal			5 000	
Annual totals			228 000	20 000
Grand total			**248 000**	

> ### Exercise
>
> Now that you have seen an example of a budget, draw up your own for your study. In the space below, jot down all the costs you anticipate relevant to the headings that have been provided.
>
> | | |
> |---|---|
> | *Staffing* | Fieldworkers _____ |
> | | Nurses _____ |
> | | Consulting fees _____ |
> | | Other _____ |
> | *Supplies* | Lab supplies (specify separately if there are several) _____ |
> | | _____ |
> | *Administration* | _____ |
> | *Travel* | Travel within the study _____ |
> | | Travel to local conferences _____ |
> | | Travel to international conferences _____ |
> | *Patient costs* | Patient care costs _____ |
> | | Reimbursements _____ |
> | *Dissemination* | Costs of publication _____ |

Timelines

You must be aware of how much time it will take for you to get the study going after getting all the required approvals, how much time it will take to gather the data, to analyse the data, and then to prepare your write-up for examination or publication. Different degrees have varying time limits, but at least one year must be allocated to preparation of the protocol and writing up the findings.

Although timelines are not often required within your protocol, in terms of budgeting your time you need to define the steps you will undertake in your research within a timescale. The times when each aspect of your study will be implemented, will run and will conclude should be indicated. Here you will place your deliverables as milestones along a timeline. One of the benefits of creating a timeline at the beginning of your study is that it will link your theoretical thinking about your research to the actual act of carrying out the study. The timeline will provide a framework in time to guide the study to ensure that it is carried out within your allotted time frame.

Budgets and timelines

The timeline will act as a check of whether or not you are going to complete your study in time and whether you are ahead or behind in your schedule at any given time. The time frame for your study may be determined by how much time your university will give you to complete the study, the amount of time your funders will give you, or the amount of time you actually have available, given that you may be doing other work while you are carrying out research.

A visual timeline will show the whole story of your research plan at a glance, succinctly emphasising the feasibility of your project.

Table 3 illustrates a visual timeline showing the progress through the study mentioned above.

Table 3: Example of a visual timeline

	Jan	Feb	March	April	May	June	July	Aug	Sep	Oct	Nov	Dec
Call 100 identified patients into the clinic for blood draw	■	■	■	■								
DNA isolation		■	■	■	■							
PCR					■	■						
Sequencing							■					
Data analysis							■	■				
Write up results for dissemination									■	■	■	■

Exercise

To do your own timeline, work out exactly how long each step in your research process will take. Then look at each process and see if it can overlap with another process; in other words, which processes can run concurrently. Now, using this information, draw up your own visual timeline in the space below.

	Jan	Feb	March	April	May	June	July	Aug	Sep	Oct	Nov	Dec

Budget and timeline checklist

- Have you checked that your application includes a template for your budget?
- If you did not receive a budget template from your institution, have you considered all aspects of your study to establish where costs could be incurred?
- Have you itemised every single process in your research plan? Ask a colleague to look at your protocol and your timeline to make sure you have not left anything out and have planned your time most expediently.
- Does your timeline fit within limits set by either funders or your institution? If your timeline exceeds the time allocated, you have to go back to the drawing board and look at your research plan.

Learning points

Time and money are limited resources within the research paradigm, and they must be managed with care. Drawing up a formal timeline and budget, which can be referred to throughout the progress of the study, will help manage these scarce resources.

The research title and your title page

The first thing reviewers see when they look at your protocol is the title. The title should set the reviewers thinking along the correct channels for the rest of your protocol. It must foreshadow the content of your protocol; that is, it should answer the reviewers' first questions: what is the research about and what can be expected from the research? If your title is not a clear indication of what the reviewer will read in the body of the protocol, you will confuse the reviewer, which will not bode well for a good review.

The title of your study will emerge after you have refined your research protocol and your aims and objectives are clear. It is only after you have spent time thinking about the study as a whole that you will have the information required for a research title. At this point it could be called a *working title*, because the title may change as the research progresses.

Here are some guidelines for writing a good title:

- The title should be short, containing 15–20 substantive words.
- It should be descriptive of what you are going to do, by making the overall aim clear.
- It should mention your variables and the study population or specific conditions of the study populations, as well as the comparisons and measurements used.
- Do not use abbreviations or rarely used acronyms and jargon in the title.
- Avoid throwaway terms such as 'analysis of', 'investigation of' etc. These terms are redundant, as all research contains some elements of investigation and analysis.
- Use well-chosen, descriptive words.

The title of your research protocol may be adapted later to become the title of one of your publications. When people use search engines to look for literature online, the search engines will pick up words from your title, so make sure it includes keywords that will attract readers to your work. Once you have reached the point where you are publishing your results, the title may change completely to reflect the results of your study.

The elements of a title will be slightly different for different types of study, but in general you need to mention the elements in the list above. Sometimes the setting and the time frame are also relevant. A good recipe to use is to write down your independent variable, your dependent variable and your study population.

Writing your first clinical research protocol

Example

Dependent variable: Peripheral arterial disease (PAD)
Independent variable: B2 microglobulin (B2M)
Study population: Patients with diabetes mellitus and varying degrees of renal function

These are all the elements that must appear in the title of the study. The title of this study could be: 'The diagnostic accuracy of B2 microglobulin (B2M) to detect peripheral arterial disease (PAD) as measured by toe blood pressure index in patients with diabetes mellitus and varying degrees of renal function.'

This is a good title because the number of variables is limited, and these are easily defined. The experiment is clearly discernible from the title. A reviewer can see that you are going to look at patients who suffer from diabetes mellitus and who have varying degrees of renal function. You are going to look at the accuracy of B2M as an indicator of PAD by measuring the blood pressure through the toes of these patients. From here on, the reviewer will know what you are doing and can grasp the rest of your protocol.

Exercise

How do you think the following titles could be improved?

1. Comparison of gated single-photon emission computed tomography with homocysteine for evaluation of myocardial ischaemia.
2. The cost of in-patients admitted to the Paediatric Intensive Care Unit (PICU) and Paediatric Pulmonology wards for treatment of Syndrome XYZ — Welkom Academic Hospital.
3. Randomised controlled trial to test heavy-load eccentric exercise for the treatment of supraspinatus tendinosis.
4. The effect of human immunodeficiency virus on the management of breast cancer.

Answers

1. The patient population being studied is not mentioned. It could be inferred that they are people evaluated for suspected myocardial ischaemia. The title could also be: 'Comparison of diagnostic characteristics between gated single-photon emission computed tomography and homocysteine in patients evaluated for possible myocardial ischaemia.'

2. For studies related to costs or prevalence/incidence, the setting and time periods are important. The title should be: 'The cost of in-patients admitted to the Paediatric Intensive Care Unit (PICU) and Paediatric Pulmonology wards for treatment of Syndrome XYZ — Welkom Academic Hospital, 2007–2009.' Costing studies vary, and from this title it is not clear whether both direct and indirect or only direct costs will be measured. This should also preferably be stated in the title.
3. The comparator is not stated. The title should rather read: 'A randomised controlled trial comparing heavy-load eccentric exercise versus … for the treatment of supraspinatus tendinosis.'
4. The words 'effect' as well as 'management' are very non-specific. The title could read (depending on the aims and objectives): 'The effect of human immunodeficiency virus status as determinant of treatment choice in women with breast cancer.' Or: 'The effect of human immunodeficiency virus status on the outcome of breast cancer as managed by …' The setting and time period should also be mentioned if this is a retro- or prospective clinical audit. If specific types or grades of breast cancer are important, they should also be mentioned.

It is helpful to write down three or four titles, ensuring that the required components are present. Then discuss these with some colleagues and your supervisor and select the best one as the title of your protocol.

Exercise

Write down two possible titles for your research project.

List the variables: _____

_____

Population: _____

Title 1: _____

_____

_____

Title 2: _____

_____

_____

✿ Writing your first clinical research protocol

The title page

The title page is the last thing you need to do when preparing your protocol document for submission. The title page requirements can vary between institutions, and some institutions have very specific requirements. Later, when you write a proposal for research funding, you may find that funding agencies also need specific information to populate your title page. Be sure to follow the instructions carefully.

Typically, the title page should have the name of your university and faculty, your research project title, your name and full contact details, the degree for which the study is required and the name and contact details of your supervisor (e-mail). Refer to Appendix A for an example of a title page.

Exercise

Check whether you have already been provided with a template for your title page from your institution. In the space below, sketch out your own title page, as prescribed in your specific template or by following the example in Appendix A.

_____

_____

_____

_____

_____

_____

_____

_____

_____

_____

_____

_____

_____

_____

The research title and your title page

Title page checklist

- Is the university name and title correct, and correctly spelt?
- Research title:
  - Does the title reflect the primary aim/objective clearly and concisely?
  - Does the title state the variables?
  - Does the title state the research population (or their condition)?
- Check student particulars, including degree.
- Check supervisor particulars.

Learning points

The title of a protocol must indicate the variables and the study population, as it serves as a starting point for reviewers' understanding of the rest of the protocol. The title is the central part of the title page and must be built in accordance with the requirements of the institution, or another appropriate template can be used.

The executive summary

An executive summary and an abstract are not the same thing. An abstract provides salient points taken from a piece of writing to tell the reader about some of the content, enough to let them decide whether or not to read the rest for detail, or discard it as irrelevant to their needs.

The purpose of an executive summary is twofold. The primary reason you write one is to give your reviewer a summary of the key points to your research, further preparing them for the upcoming content. It gives a fuller picture of the entire study, after the title has given them the initial idea. It also provides a recapitulation that can be read after the entire protocol has been perused, and which will help the reviewer to clearly understand your study.

The executive summary should provide your central thesis, with a few crucial details so that it can be read in isolation in order to understand the study.

You may be given an indication of the length of the executive summary by your institution, but a rule of thumb is that it should not exceed 10% of the length of the entire document. Therefore, for a report spanning 5 000 words, your executive summary would not exceed 500 words.

Another good reason for an executive summary is that it helps you clarify the essential issues from the start. The executive summary should answer the questions why, what and how, as well as describe the potential output and impact of the project. It does not contain references (as an abstract might) and is short. The executive summary answers the following important questions:

- Why is this project necessary?
- What are you going to do?
- How are you going to do the project?
- What is the potential impact of the project? How will the research findings change our way of thinking or doing things?

Example of a good executive summary

Study title: The diagnostic accuracy of B2 microglobulin (B2M) to detect peripheral arterial disease (PAD) as measured by toe blood pressure index in patients with diabetes mellitus and varying degrees of renal function.

The executive summary

Peripheral arterial disease is an important complication to detect in patients with diabetes mellitus. Screening and diagnosis typically involve ultrasound (costly and time-consuming). This study aims to determine whether serum B2 microglobulin (a blood test) can predict peripheral arterial disease in patients with diabetes and varying degrees of reduced glomerular filtration rates. Toe blood pressure indices will be measured with a photo-plethysmograph. Demographic clinical variables, as well as serum B2M, Cystatin C, C-reactive protein (CRP), serum creatinine, serum lipids and HbA1c will be collected. The use of a biomarker for peripheral arterial disease may overcome the many limitations of current tests to identify this condition and could facilitate earlier diagnosis and management.

Excercise

Having seen a good executive summary, read the following two summaries critically:

Executive summary 1

Percutaneous biopsy of chest and abdominal masses with the use of CT guidance has become a well-established method in recent years. Fine needle aspiration is one technique frequently used but can only provide cytological and not histological results. Larger tissue samples can be harvested using a core needle biopsy, thereby allowing for assessment of tissue architecture. Increased rates of pneumothoraces and other complications are associated with this procedure because the biopsy needles are larger in diameter.

This retrospective study aims to examine 200 patients at Harrismith Hospital who have had CT guided biopsies from January 2007 until July 2010 (2.5 years) and report the adequacy of biopsy specimens and the complication rate.

How do you think this executive summary could be improved?

_____
_____
_____
_____
_____

Executive summary 2

Macro- and microvascular complications in the diabetic population often lead to the need for lower extremity amputations after conservative measures have failed.[1] Surgical site infection is a known postoperative complication after lower extremity amputations.[2] Predicting which diabetic patients pre-operatively are at an increased risk for developing a surgical site infection after a lower extremity amputation could lead to possible timely preventative measures.

Measuring glycated haemoglobin (HbA1c) pre-operatively of diabetics requiring a lower extremity amputation, and correlating the level of glycaemic control with the development of a surgical site infection, could reveal which patients are at increased risk. It is the perception in our hospital that diabetic patients are more likely to develop a surgical site infection after lower extremity amputations. Previous studies revealed the poor glycaemic control of the South African diabetic population, which increases their risk for requiring amputations and possibly increasing the risk for surgical site infections.[3-5]

This study could place emphasis on the importance of tight early glycaemic control in the diabetic population, decreasing complication rates, with fewer patients requiring lower extremity amputations. Furthermore, this study will help in identifying patients pre-operatively as high-risk individuals for surgical site infection with more aggressive treatment (surgical and medical) with a decrease in the incidence of surgical site infections. Shorter hospital stays will decrease hospital costs, while the absence of surgical site infections will allow earlier rehabilitation, with improvement of quality of life, and a decrease in the financial burden on society.

Write down what you think about this summary.

_____
_____
_____
_____
_____

See the end of this section for suggestions regarding both summaries.

The executive summary

Pitfalls to avoid

- The executive summary is often confused with an abstract. Be clear on the difference.
- Make sure the executive summary is the right length. Do not make it too long or too short.
- Make sure all the who, what, why and how questions are addressed. Do not leave anything out.
- Do not use references in this section.

Exercise

Now write your own executive summary for your research project. Remember the following:

- State the problem.
- State what you plan to do and how you are going to do it.
- State what the potential impact of this research would be.
- Be clear and concise.

Start by writing down one sentence for each of the following questions:

- Why is this project necessary?

  _____

- What are you going to do?

  _____

- How are you going to do the project?

  _____

- What is the potential impact of the project? How will the research findings change our way of thinking or doing things?

  _____

Now expand on your sentences, if necessary, for explanation and clarity.

_____

_____

_____

_____

Take your points and supporting sentences and write them up as a story, ensuring that the story conveys your research ideas clearly. A reviewer must be able to skim-read the summary and know exactly what is going to happen in the rest of the protocol.

_____
_____
_____
_____
_____
_____
_____

Suggestions on how to improve executive summaries 1 and 2

For executive summary 1:

This summary does not give any motivation as to why this study is needed or of what use the results will be. The value of the study is not specified at all (output and impact are not mentioned).

For executive summary 2:

This summary is everything but clear and concise. The problem is stated, but the summary is too long. An executive summary should not include references. Using words such as 'could' do not really convince the reader about the potential impact. There is no clear indication what the actual study entails. There is no summary of the protocol in this executive summary. The final paragraph regarding costs is beyond the scope of this study.

Executive summary checklist

✻ Have you included answers to all the why, what and how questions? Potential impact and output questions? ➲

The executive summary

- Have you remained within the word limit for your executive summary (either a predetermined word limit or 10% of your entire script)?
- Have you made sure there are no references in the executive summary?
- Can a colleague get the gist of your project by reading the executive summary? It is always good to get peer review done on things like the executive summary.

Learning points

The executive summary is a précis of the entire protocol. The purpose is to provide the reader with an overall idea of what the entire protocol contains. It provides more information than an abstract would and is written in a less technical way. It is an abridged version of the entire protocol that can stand alone as a document to represent the entire protocol.

Reporting your findings and establishing authorship

The dissemination of your findings, although not often a fixed requirement in your protocol, is an important part of your research. Spreading the word about your findings is your academic and social responsibility. How are you going to make the results of your research known to others who may be affected or influenced by it? This will include your study participants (as a courtesy), possibly the public at large, public health departments and policy makers, as well as colleagues in the academic world, who can then use your work to inform their own work. If you plan your dissemination strategy early on in your study, you will avoid a haphazard scramble at the end. There is always the risk that new knowledge will become stagnant unless it is mobilised to where it will do good.

The means of disseminating your research findings may include the following:

- Newsletters read by authorities, policy makers or interested communities;
- Workshops for other researchers, policy makers or authorities;
- Public presentations as a guest speaker;
- Professional conference presentations;
- Popular media releases;
- Internet sites featuring topics relevant to your research; and
- Academic journal articles.

Different methods of dissemination will be more appropriate for the different audiences you need to inform. Your patients are not likely to read an academic journal article. A workshop, or a letter sent out to each patient directly (accompanied by an expression of thanks for their participation), may be more appropriate. If your results prove to have an enormous impact on health, you may want to shout them from the rooftops in the form of newspaper articles or radio and TV releases.

None of these should happen before your results have been published in an academic journal. The peer review that occurs prior to publication will give you the confidence to disseminate your findings without compunction. Most journals will not publish anything that has already been released to the public. So, the first step in your plan for the dissemination of your research findings will be to decide which journal you will publish in. By thinking about which journals you want to publish your work in before you start writing, you will save time in getting your material written in the correct format for those journals from the start.

Reporting your findings and establishing authorship

Drawing up a dissemination plan

The best way to design your dissemination plan is to look at who should be made aware of your research findings and which is the most appropriate method to deliver the findings to them. A matrix, like the example in Table 4, can be very useful.

Table 4: Dissemination matrix

	Journal article	Conference	Workshops	Newsletters	Popular media	Public presentation	Other (specify)
The academic world	yes	yes					
Study participants			yes	yes			
The general public					yes	yes	
Public health departments/ policy makers			yes	yes			

Your own dissemination plan matrix could look different. The scale of your study may be so small that you do not anticipate a release of the findings to the general public. Your study participants may be illiterate, so sending them a newsletter may be futile. In their case, a workshop would be a better bet.

Exercise

Use the following template to list those parties to whom your results should be disseminated.

	Journal article	Confer-ence	Work-shops	News-letters	Popular media	Public presentation	Other (specify)
The academic world							
Study participants							
The general public							
Public health departments/ policy makers							

Writing your first clinical research protocol

Authorship

Establishing who will get authorship on any publications is best decided before the study begins. This will prevent uncomfortable situations later when you are due to publish. There are criteria that must be fulfilled for someone to be included in the list of authors on a paper. These criteria are established along strict ethical lines and should not be ignored. It is unethical for someone to be included as an author on a paper if he or she does not fulfil the minimum requirements for authorship.

If a prospective author has made substantial contributions to the intellectual content of your paper in all the following three categories (tick at least one option in each category), then they are eligible for co-authorship:

1. Conception and design of the research project
   Acquisition of the data
   Analysis and interpretation of the data
2. Drafting the article
   Revising it critically for important intellectual content
3. Statistical analysis
   Obtaining funding
   Administrative, technical or material support
   Supervision
   Other (specify)

It is clear, therefore, that a supervisor is not eligible to be a co-author unless he or she can tick at least one action in each category. It is also clear from these guidelines that 'guest' authorship would be considered unethical. All authors should provide you with permission to include them in your journal article writing exercise.

There may be some people who play an important part in your study but are not able to tick off an action in each of the three sections. These people must be given due recognition of their inputs by being acknowledged in the Acknowledgements section in any papers emanating from work they may have assisted in. Such people could include statisticians, technicians and researchers. Right to authorship is not tied to position or to payment.

Exercise

Use the following matrix to list your proposed authors, and stipulate their roles in your article writing later. Remember to get permission from each author before you include their names in your matrix. Tick off the actions you will expect of them in each of the categories.

Reporting your findings and establishing authorship

Author	Category 1			Category 2		Category 3				
	Conception and design of the research project	Acquisition of the data	Analysis and interpretation of the data	Drafting the article	Revising it critically for important intellectual content	Statistical analysis	Obtaining funding	Administrative, technical or material support	Supervision	Other
1 (You)										
2										
3										
4										
5										

You may want to carry out similar exercises for the other modes of dissemination. For example, you might want to involve your fieldworkers in running workshops to disseminate findings to your study participants, or you may want your supervisor to speak to the media on your behalf if you are desperately shy of the public eye.

Learning points

Making research results known to everyone who could be affected by them is a responsibility for the researcher, as well as an integral part of the research process. The academic article is a gateway to broader dissemination of findings in that the peer review system acts as a quality control for research. Once research findings have been accepted as sound by the scientific community, they should be disseminated to all other affected parties, which could include the research participants, others in your organisation and the general public, if appropriate.

References and appendices

This final section of your protocol preparation involves very little deep thought, but it is surprising how many protocols are sent back to students because the referencing is inaccurate and not all the appendices are provided. Ensuring that your reference list is accurate and that all the requested appendices are included as requested (even in the order in which they have been requested) is not difficult to do, but can take some time to put together properly. This step is worth taking time over to ensure that accuracy is achieved.

References

Referencing in your text was addressed earlier, in the section on literature reviews. Let us focus now on the list of references that will occur at the end of your writing. This is the list of all the literature you have cited. Simple. So make sure that all the works are cited in this list and that all the references cited in this list actually do appear in the text. If you have been using referencing software such as EndNote, there should be no problem. As you worked through your text, adding and removing citations over time, the software would have kept track of the changes, and all references in the text should appear in your list of references.

However, if you have been working manually, you will have to spend some time checking your text and your list. Luckily, in the age of computers, you can use the 'Find' function within a document. You can work through your reference list while 'finding' the authors throughout the text. If a name does not occur in the text, it is likely that you edited their citation out of your writing at some point and forgot to remove the citation from the list of references, or that it was spelled differently in the text and list of references.

What you also have to do is check that all the citations within your text occur in the reference list. To do this, you will have to read your text with the reference list on hand and tick off each citation on the reference list as you find it in the text. If you cannot find 'Adams et al' in your reference list and it is in your introduction, you know to add that entry now.

Once you have established that all your references are in the list of references and all the entries in the list of references are actually in the text, you have to check each citation slowly and pedantically to ensure that they are correctly presented as per the format that you have been asked to use. For example, if your format requires that you write 'Adams & Eva', make sure you have not written 'Adams and Eva' anywhere. You must check through your text with a fine-tooth comb to make sure all citations

References and appendices

are correct. The same holds for your list of references. Ensure that the dates are in the correct place, that full stops occur where they should and that italics or bold are appropriately used. You will have all these rules either given to you, or you would have found them on the internet when you started writing.

Once again, this step is obviated if you use referencing software. So, it is gently suggested that you learn to use at least one referencing software package before you start writing. The time spent in becoming familiar with the program is well invested. You will be particularly grateful later in your career when you have an article returned to you from one journal (which uses referencing format A) suggesting that you send it to another more appropriate journal (which uses referencing format B). If you use your referencing software, the change from one format to the other is instantaneous. On the other hand, having to do a manual change could put you off resubmitting to the second journal.

Appendices

Many institutions require additional information to accompany your protocol submission. These could include your CV, the CV of your supervisor, a copy of the information which will be given to study participants, a copy of your informed consent document (in all the languages in which it will be presented), a copy of your study instrument, a copy of your proof of registration as a student, a list of consultants who might be involved in the study and a copy of the written permission you have obtained to conduct the research at a specific site. You may be required to provide certified copies of certain documentation. You may also be required to provide the signature of your supervisor or any other involved party. These instructions will be provided to you by the organisation to whom you are submitting your protocol. It is a good idea to list their requirements and then tick them off as you put each piece together.

Exercise

Write down all the appendices and signatures that you are required to submit by the institution. Then cross them off as you add them to your documentation.

_____

_____

_____

_____

Writing your first clinical research protocol

> *Learning points*
>
> The final part of putting the protocol together for submission involves ensuring that all references are present and correct in both the text and the list of references, and that all requested appendices are provided in the format requested.

Bibliography

Department of Health. South African Good Clinical Practice Guidelines, 2006. Available from www.doh.gov.za/docs/factsheets/guidelines/clinical/2006/index.html; accessed 9 June 2011.

Emanuel E, Wendler D, Grady C. What makes clinical research ethical? *Journal of the American Medical Association* 2000;283(20):2701–11.

Joubert G, Ehrlich R (eds). 2007. *Epidemiology: a Research Manual for South Africa*. 2nd ed. Cape Town: Oxford University Press Southern Africa.

Knottnerus J, Van Weel C, Muris J. Evaluation of diagnostic procedures. *British Medical Journal* 2002;324:477–80.

Sackett D, Hayes R. The architecture of diagnostic research. *British Medical Journal* 2000;324:539–41.

Appendix A: An example of a protocol template

University of Pretoria
Faculty of Health Sciences
School of Medicine

Title
(must be short and concise and reflect your primary aim; use Title Case)

Degree: (for example, MMed Surgery)

Author:
Student no:

Contact details:

Address:

Tel:

Fax:

Cell:

E-mail:

Supervisor: (name)
E-mail address:

Co-supervisor: (name if relevant, otherwise delete)
22 June 2011

Executive summary

This must answer the following questions (but don't include the actual questions in the summary, and please note: no references in the executive summary):

- Why is this project necessary?

Appendix A: An example of a protocol template

- What are you going to do?
- How are you going to do the project?
- What are the project outputs?
- What is the impact of the project?

Table of contents

1. Defining the research problem	5
2. Literature overview and motivation	5
3. Aim and objectives	5
4. Methods	6
4.1. Study design	6
4.2. Setting	6
4.3. Patient/research object selection	6
4.4. Measurements	6
4.5. Data analysis	6
4.5.1. Sample size	7
5. Ethical considerations	7
6. Budget	7
7. Timelines and project management	7
8. Contributors and authorship	7
9. References	8
10. Appendices	10

1. Defining the research problem

This gives a brief overview of the research problem (maximum 2–3 paragraphs). For example: TB in the age group 3–6 years is increasing disproportionately to other age groups. Various risk factors have been identified but the role of day-care centres has not been investigated.

2. Literature overview and motivation

Content will be determined according to your protocol, but should include the following (don't use as subheadings):

- Historical background
- Why is this subject important?
- What is known from previous studies?
- Critically appraise and show limitations of previous studies, if any
- What factors (and why) led to the research project?

Writing your first clinical research protocol

- Justification/relevance/impact of your study (based on the above aspects: for example, importance of subject, gaps in knowledge, request from the institution, what the anticipated impact of the research may be etc)

3. Aim and objectives

For example:

Aim: To investigate risk factors for TB in children aged 3–6 years in Limpopo Province

Objectives:
1. To determine the relationship between birth weight and development of TB at the age of 3–6 yrs
2. To determine the relationship between day care, type of care giver and TB …
3. To determine the relationship between socio-demographic factors and TB …

Alternatively, in the case of an analytical/experimental study, use the following:

Hypothesis: Our hypothesis is that the type of day-care centre is associated with risk of TB in children between 3–6 years old.

4. Methods

4.1. Study design

For example: Observational, cross-sectional

4.2. Setting

For example: Tertiary care dermatology clinic

4.3. Patient/research object selection

Sampling strategy and sampling frame, if relevant, *or* patient selection/recruitment, including inclusion and exclusion criteria, randomisation and blinding procedures, if relevant.

4.4. Measurements

Here you mention what you are going to measure (the variables), how you are going to measure these (including definitions, if relevant) and what steps you are going to take to avoid measurement error (random and systematic error).

Appendix A: An example of a protocol template

4.5. Data analysis

Here you often need statistical advice.

For example: Descriptive statistics will be used to describe the sample, and paired T-tests will be used to compare the blood pressure before and after exercise. A P value of < 0.05 will be regarded as statistically significant.

4.5.1. Sample size

Here you most definitely need statistical advice.

For example: To detect a clinically significant difference of 5 mm Hg between pre- and post-exercise with an alpha value of 0.05 and a power of 90%, 33 subjects are required.

5. Ethical considerations

What are the ethical issues of importance in your study and how will they be addressed? Are you obtaining informed consent (specify detail)? To which committee(s) are you applying for approval?

6. Budget

Item description	Cost	
Total project cost		

7. Timelines and project management

Here you could include a Gantt chart and details as to how the project will be managed.

8. Contributors and authorship

Name	Department	Contribution	Author or acknowledgement

9. References

Only use the Vancouver style: see http://0-www.lib.monash.edu.au.innopac.up.ac.za/tutorials/citing/vancouver.html. Include a maximum of three website references.

10. Appendices

This should include your questionnaire/informed consent, letters of approval etc.

Index

abstracts 68
accuracy 30
aims and objectives 14–17
Algorithm for choice of statistical test for independent groups 53
analytical studies 12, 24
APA style 19
appendices 79
authorship 76–77

bias 32
biostatistics 1
budgets 57–59

case-control studies 25
categorical variables 47
checklists
    aims and objectives 17
    budgets 62
    executive summaries 72–73
    literature review 23
    R-E-F-I-N-E 12–13
    research focus 10
    research problem 12
    S-M-A-R-T 13
    timelines 62
    title page 67
citations 18–19, 78–79
    APA style 19
    Harvard style 19
    literature review 22
    tutorials for 19
    Vancouver style 18–19
clinical trials 26–27, 55
cohort studies 25, 55
Components of error 31
confounding bias 32
Consort Statement 27
cross-sectional studies 25

data analysis 47, 55
data collection 43–44
databases 1
decision tree 25–26
dependent variables 50–51, 53

descriptive studies 12, 24
diagnostic studies 55
dichotomous key 51–54
Dichotomous key for statistical test selection 52–53
Dissemination matrix 75
dissemination plan 74–75
DV see dependent variables

electronic management 19
    literature sources 19
    referencing software 78, 79
epidemiologic studies 55
ethics 40–41
Example of non-normal distribution 49
Example of normal distribution 49
Example of research budget 58–59
Example of visual timeline 61
Example of the effect of confounding in the association between independent variable and dependent variable 51
executive summaries 68–70
expenses 57–58

Good Clinical Practice (GCP) 41
Google Scholar 6

Harvard style 19
hypotheses 12

incidence 24
Independent and paired groups research designs 50
independent groups 50, 53
independent variables 50–51, 53
information bias 32
interventional/experimental studies 24, 26
IV see independent variables

keywords 63

limitations 45
list of references 78–79
literature review 1, 18–23
    checklist 23

citations 22
 organising of 20
 pitfalls 21–22
 purpose of 18
 structure of 20
 tips 21
literature sources 19

matched groups *see* paired groups
measurement 31
measurement error 31
measurement statements 32

NHREC's online ethics application system 27
non-normal distributions 48–49
normal distributions 48–49
numerical variables 47

observational studies 24, 25–26

paired groups 50
plagiarism 18
precision 31
presentation skills 2
prevalence 24

questionnaires 43
questions, focused 1

random errors 31
randomised clinical trials 25, 26
reference techniques *see* citations
referencing software 78, 79
referencing styles *see* citations
R-E-F-I-N-E 12–13
reliability 43
research constraints 2–3
research findings 74–75
research focus 5–8, 10
research objectives 25

research problems
 defining of 8
 pitfalls 9
research problem statements 9
 reasons why 11
 R-E-F-I-N-E 12–13
 S-M-A-R-T 13
research protocol
 development of 3
 example of 82–86
research questions 12
 phrasing of 17
sample size 36, 55
 calculation of 37–39
sampling 34
sampling, types of 35
scales of measurement 47–48
scientific writing 1
selection bias 32
S-M-A-R-T 13
STARD Statement 27
statistical tests 51–54
study design 24
 limitations 45–46
 types of 25
study populations 34
survival analysis 55
systematic errors 31

theoretical populations 34
timelines 60–61
title 63
 examples of 64
 guidelines for 63
 keywords 63
title page 66

validity 32, 43
Vancouver style 18–19
variables 44